GW01045906

How I
Liberated
Burgundy

By the same author

Madly in All Directions

The Shell Guide to Wales (with Alan Llewelyn)

The Splendour Falls

Portrait of Gower

The Countryside Companion

Secret Landscapes

Trust to Talk

Wynford Vaughan-Thomas's Wales

The Princess of Wales

Wales: A History

How I Liberated Burgundy

and Other Vinous Adventures

'Vineyard' Vaughan-Thomas

Line drawings by Derek Crowe

MICHAEL JOSEPH
London

First published in Great Britain by Michael Joseph Ltd
44 Bedford Square, London WC1
1985

© Wynford Vaughan-Thomas 1985

Line drawings copyright © Derek Crowe

All Rights Reserved. No part of this publication may be
reproduced, stored in a retrieval system, or transmitted
in any form or by any means, electronic, mechanical,
photocopying, recording or otherwise, without the prior
permission of the Copyright owner.

British Library Cataloguing in Publication Data

Vaughan-Thomas, Wynford
How I liberated Burgundy:
and other vinous adventures.
1. Vaughan-Thomas, Wynford
2. Broadcasters — Great Britain — Biography
I. Title
791.44'092'4   PN1990.72.V/

ISBN 0-7181-2641-6

Printed in Great Britain by
Hollen Street Press Ltd at Slough

The poem on page 113 is from
Collected Poems by Dylan Thomas,
published by J. M. Dent & Sons, Ltd

CONTENTS

PREFACE

It was the late André Simon, that prince among the pro-
tagonists of the wines of his native France, who re-christened
me 'Vineyard' Vaughan-Thomas. Throughout his long residence in London he retained his charming French accent, and
Celtic names – especially Welsh ones – present impossible
problems to French speakers. How does a Frenchman tackle
the – to him – totally improbable juxtaposition of 'W' and 'y'
in my name? André solved it by addressing me as 'Mon cher
Vineyard'. I accepted this happy improvisation with pride. I
felt I had earned it by the part I played in helping to save some
of the greatest vineyards of France in August 1944. I had
landed with the French army in the south of France, near St
Tropez, on a warm late summer's morning. We chased the
retreating Germans out of a succession of noble names, from
Châteauneuf-du-Pape to Hermitage. We gave them no time to
carry out a 'scorched earth' policy on the precious vineyards,
and won our greatest triumph when we liberated the Golden
Slope of Burgundy itself. Not a tank track crushed the orderly
rows of the great vines of Meursault, Beaune and Nuits-Saint-
Georges. Could this, after all, be the greatest unsung victory of
the war?

André agreed with me that the Liberation of Burgundy was a
major turning point in the great struggle to save civilisation. A
few years after the war we were lunching together and
discussing the merits of a 1945 burgundy. I was rash enough to
maintain – after a third glass – that but for me we would not
have been enjoying this rare bottled nectar. A slight exag-
geration, of course, for the whole French army also had

vii

something to do with it, but I was the BBC War Correspondent on the spot. I had the microphone, and when it comes to writing modern history, the man who counts is the man who has quick personal access to the powers of publicity!

'You must write the story,' declared André, and I naturally agreed. But I kept on postponing the delightful task – I must have been too busy building up my post-war cellar. Somehow the years slipped by and I still hadn't put pen to paper. Now that we have celebrated VE day and we have all been on nostalgic journeys back into our wartime past, I feel I have no further excuse. It is now or never. To inspire me, I went down to the cellar and decanted a bottle of burgundy of the VE year, a 1945 Corton, Clos du Roi. Yes, I still have a few bottles of such wine left. As far as I can see, there are only two advantages about the business of growing older. You can travel half-fare on British Rail, and you had the chance to lay down great wines before their prices had taken off into outer financial space and made them the exclusive preserve of American millionaires and Japanese businessmen.

Old wine is always a calculated gamble; it can let you down in front of your friends. In that case the only thing to do is to harden your heart and pour it down the drain after steaming off the label as a pious memorial to that which was once great. But this bottle

viii

of burgundy simply got up and sang. The first glass demanded all those esoteric analyses about bouquet, body, staying power and the rest of it which arouse the derision of the swilling brigade – those happy innocents who declare that they know what they like and proceed to prove it by drinking anything with everything. They deserve those brightly labelled containers of glorified vinegar sold in certain pubs and supermarkets which shall be mercifully nameless.

My noble bottle was in another class altogether, but perhaps the inspiration it supplied was a little too generous. I set out to write a sober account of the campaign, but how can you use such a word as sober when you are dealing with wine? Now, after many months and many other bottles, I contemplate the result with a certain pleased dismay. My little book set out with the best of intentions. I had hoped to tell the story in sequence, but somehow or other I have yielded to temptation on the way. I have remembered many a delicious story inspired by wine, and almost before I realise it, there it is happily enshrined in my deviating narrative. As I look back I seem to have written, not only an account of the Liberation of Burgundy, but also my own vinous autobiography – the Confessions of a Civilised Imbiber.

Yet, come to think of it, doesn't this exactly reflect the spirit of the whole campaign: surprises, sidetracks, seductive diversions – a splendidly wobbly progress up the Rhône valley to arrive at last at the supreme objective, the Decanting of Burgundy.

So let us set off in the spirit of the old French proverb: 'It is better to travel hopefully than to arrive.' But still confident that eventually we will be safe somewhere in a cellar on the Côte d'Or, drinking without doubt a Richebourg '34. But first, *'Garçon, une autre bouteille!'*

CHAPTER ONE

The Art of Civilized Drinking

It seems a long time ago – over forty years back as I write this – but I still have vivid memories of the first bottle of wine I drank after I had landed with the French army in the south of France on 15 August 1944. I wish I could claim that it was a noble bottle, worthy of the occasion. It was nothing of the sort. It was a strong Provençal wine, of nondescript origin, but presented to me free by a café owner in a little village behind St Tropez, who had been carried away by the excitement of finding himself suddenly liberated.

Now, even the French experts don't glow with enthusiasm when they discuss the wines of Provence and Languedoc. '*Les vins du Midi,*' they pontificate, '*on les avale; on ne les déguste pas.*' In other words, you don't savour the wines of the south of France, you just gulp 'em down. But the pundits who advise you on how to judge wine always leave out one important element in your enjoyment of a bottle – the time and the place where you drink it. Even in Benidorm, a bottle of 'plonk' in the right atmosphere can taste like Château Latour.

I learnt that lesson in the days before the war when it was still possible to get into a car and drive across the Continent as far as the Black Sea if you wanted to.

A friend and I set off on this delightful journey and eventually drove into Budapest – long before the Iron Curtain was even dreamt of. We found ourselves entertaining two delightful young Hungarian ladies in a café on Margaret Island and drinking wines from Lake Balaton. I have never drunk any Hungarian wines since, but they live in my memory as nectar for the gods.

A total illusion of course, but it was a starlit night, there was a gypsy violinist plucking at our heartstrings and a cimbalom player tinkling up and down the scales. This was the Hungary of popular romance with not a detail missing. And I wasn't surprised when, later at dawn, my friend found himself in the flat with one of the young ladies who had obviously granted him her supreme favours. He was no Adonis and could not help asking, as he gave her his grateful thanks, 'How can I express my gratitude? Why have you been so kind to me?' She smiled up at him, 'But it was to improve my English.' After that, we both decided that, as we could never be great lovers, we might as well be great wine-lovers.

That bottle of Provençal wine had the same romantic aura to me as the Balaton wines I had drunk in Budapest. Again the quality of the wines did not matter. The time and the place were right. After all, we had just come ashore in the easiest landing of the whole war. We had put down a tremendous

barrage and dashed for the shore, expecting to be mown down by machine-guns. Not a single bullet whistled past us: the Germans had tactfully pulled out a few hours before, and in their place an immaculately dressed Frenchman advanced out of the dust of war. He carried a tray with a magnum of champagne and ten glasses. The war in our sector stopped immediately. '*Soyez les bienvenus*,' he beamed in welcome. Then he added, 'Yes, welcome, gentlemen, welcome; but if I may venture a little criticism, you *are* four years late!'

Four years late or not – it didn't matter. We drove rapidly inland. On that August day, the whole of Provence seemed to be offering itself to us free.

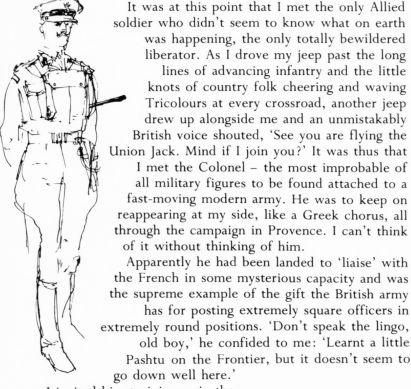

It was at this point that I met the only Allied soldier who didn't seem to know what on earth was happening, the only totally bewildered liberator. As I drove my jeep past the long lines of advancing infantry and the little knots of country folk cheering and waving Tricolours at every crossroad, another jeep drew up alongside me and an unmistakably British voice shouted, 'See you are flying the Union Jack. Mind if I join you?' It was thus that I met the Colonel – the most improbable of all military figures to be found attached to a fast-moving modern army. He was to keep on reappearing at my side, like a Greek chorus, all through the campaign in Provence. I can't think of it without thinking of him.

Apparently he had been landed to 'liaise' with the French in some mysterious capacity and was the supreme example of the gift the British army has for posting extremely square officers in extremely round positions. 'Don't speak the lingo, old boy,' he confided to me: 'Learnt a little Pashtu on the Frontier, but it doesn't seem to go down well here.'

I invited him to join me in the nearby café, where the proprietor had spotted our British uniforms and was already preparing a meal for the brave liberators. It would be free. How sadly I feel the contrast these days when I go to France, where the restaurateurs cannot wait to slap the bill before you when they find out that you are English. All old liberators will

know the feeling. But on that mellow afternoon in August 1944, bills were an irrelevance. With that bottle of Provençal wine before us, I could contemplate my new acquaintance with the interest of a biologist contemplating a new specimen. We shall not see his like again. The Raj has disappeared into the mists of history, and by no stretch of the imagination can I see him fitting into the streamlined, professional British army of today. He admitted that he had arrived at the south of France landing by the old-fashioned way of 'knowing a pal in the War House who'd served with me in India, old boy. Got back home in '39 when this little bit of bother blew up. Had to get into it, of course.'

At that moment the proprietor proudly laid the main course before us – a rich dish which I did not quite recognise but which tasted delicious. We tucked in with gusto, and at last sat back happily to sample the cognac. Our host enquired anxiously if we had enjoyed our meal. We assented vigorously and the proprietor beamed. *'Ah, je vois, messieurs, que vous êtes les hippophages?'* 'What does he say?' asked the Colonel. I had to take the risk of translating. 'He asks if we are keen horse-meat eaters.' 'Good God,' spluttered the Colonel, 'I've been eating horse; and my brother's an MFH!'

He had committed the supreme sin of the horse-lover. He had eaten his beloved. It was worse than cannibalism. It took several applications of cognac before he recovered his equilibrium. Then he remarked, philosophically, 'Well, what can you expect when you are grabbing a bit of loot.'

The word 'loot' startled me. I admit that one of the main pleasures that I was anticipating after the landing was the marvellous chance of sampling the great wines of France. This campaign would complete my vinous education, for there is no doubt about it – a wine tasting is always most successful when you arrive at the cellar door in a tank flying the Tricolour and accompanied by a cheering crowd. But that word 'loot' stirred my conscience. Surely it wouldn't apply to those voluntary offerings of noble vintages which I felt sure would come my way once we were clear of the Provençal vineyards? Surely this would be gentlemanly liberation, not loot!

The Colonel quickly solved the problem. 'Easy; only officers liberate – other ranks loot.' He had something there. We both agreed that all armies, Allied and German, loot at the moment of victory. After the horror and turmoil of battle, a dam breaks and the victorious troops tend to grab everything of value in sight. Prisoners recognise this on both sides. As you put up your hands in surrender you expect to lose your wristwatch.

You are safely out of it but the victors have to go on and fight again. And what makes them fight? At this point, the Colonel started quoting that ruthless realist, Kipling:

'Ow the loot!
Bloomin' loot!
That's the thing that makes the boys get up an' shoot!'

7

Late Victorian society was shocked by this outspoken spilling of the beans, but they consoled themselves by agreeing with Kipling that looting was strictly a matter for the rank and file. Officers only accepted gifts given in gratitude for their chivalrous conduct towards the defeated. I accepted the Colonel's definition and the Victorian judgement. Yes, I was a liberator and not a looter, and must now confess that I had already been trying my hand at the business before I landed in the south of France. I had been in the Italian campaign – dramatic curtain-raiser for the greater task of the Liberation of Burgundy.

I came out to Italy as a BBC War Correspondent. I arrived after the Salerno landing and found the Allied armies stuck in the mountains just north of Naples. Winter was approaching. Sunny Italy was becoming distinctly unsunny, and to add to the general malaise, General Montgomery was about to leave the Italian theatre to take charge of the Second Front. He gave a final interview to the correspondents as we waited outside his HQ caravan at Vasto in a rain that steadily increased as we waited. At last, the familiar bereted figure stepped briskly out of the caravan.

'Gentlemen, I've called you here to say that I am leaving to organise the Second Front. It will be a success. I shall be in charge.' The rain seemed to become wetter still. 'But I want you to be absolutely certain of one thing – my men, the splendid men of my 8th Army – they've got their tails well up! Yes, well up!' An American correspondent behind me had the courage to ask the test question, 'Excuse me, General, up what?' Monty turned on his heel and went back to his caravan.

Up what, indeed? The Germans were firmly dug in along the Gustav Line in the mountains, behind the seemingly impregnable barrier of Monte Cassino. Snow was already forming on the high peaks, and no one quite knew what to do next. There was an undeniable malaise in the air. As far as I was concerned, there was a secret source for this depression which never appeared in the military analyses: we were stuck in the south of Italy, that part of the country which could rival Provence and Languedoc in the art of producing bad wine. It was all the greater shock to me since I had cherished, from my schooldays, a romantic picture of southern Italy as a sort of vinous paradise.

It was all the fault of the splendidly out-of-date education I received at Swansea Grammar School in the 1920s. The whole curriculum seemed designed to fit us all for a scholarship to Oxford, after which we would naturally become top-level civil servants, barristers, doctors, or even enter the Church. Certainly, none of our masters seemed to contemplate their pupils entering industry or the strange world of PR and the rest of the new 'in' occupations of our mechanised, plastic age. When I look back on my education, I have an uneasy feeling that I am as much a curiosity in modern society as the Colonel! We still felt that a classical education was the best possible preparation for success in life.

How innocent we were – almost as innocent as our classics master himself, a charming, absent-minded scholar who had not the slightest idea of discipline in the classroom! His mind was always concentrated on his next learned contribution to the *Classical Review*. One lunchtime the class spent the whole break rigging lines of almost invisible black cotton to every lamp in the room. When the master returned and took his place at the desk, the signal was given, the lamps set swinging, and amid a furious banging of desks, the whole class shouted, 'Look out, earthquake, sir, earthquake!' The master looked up and said mildly, 'Ah, yes, indeed, an earthquake. Now this gives me the opportunity to remind you of the felicity of Virgil's description of this curious phenomenon. Let me see – yes, Williams, will you remind the class of the quotation?' No doubt about it, our classics master was also a master of the felicitous aside.

By the time I
had landed in
Italy, I had long
forgotten the finer
points of Latin
grammar that
he had tried
so hard to
din into me,
but I had
vivid memories
of the great discourse
he once gave the class on
the wines of Greece and Rome.
'What was the Greeks' greatest
contribution to civilisation?'
he asked us.

Like a lot of little swots anxious to say
the right thing, we produced all the obvious answers from the
Parthenon to Plato, Homer, Sophocles and Aeschylus – in fact,
any prominent Greek name we could remember. The classics
master gave a quizzical smile. 'You are all wrong, gentlemen.
The Greeks invented the wine stopper. They were thus the
first to make vintage wine.'

He went on to expound the curious story
of the Greek discovery that, if you kept
fine wines in carefully sealed airtight
earthenware containers or *amphorae*, they
would keep for years and improve as they
aged. Other ancient people had made wine,
including the Egyptians and the Hebrews –
the Old Testament is full of references to
wine making glad the heart of man, a
counsel old Noah took, with disastrous
results. But there is no indication that
Jehovah was offered vintage wine.

There are disturbing pieces of evidence to the contrary. What about that huge cluster of grapes called Eshcol, celebrated in Numbers xiii, 24, that was such a heavy symbol of fertility that it took two men to carry it on a staff! Such a piece of vinous vulgarity would never have been countenanced by the Greek wine-growers who had early learned the value of the pruning knife. In addition, they were master potters, using only the best clay and thus making certain that their amphorae were airtight.

The Romans inherited the Greek art of vintage wine-making. Our classics master fairly glowed with secret pleasure when he rolled the names of the great Roman wines over his tongue. He almost seemed to have tasted them himself. He proclaimed that the greatest of them all was the Falernian, produced in the Neapolitan *campagna*, well south of Rome. 'You remember Horace praised it,' he reminded us, 'and surely Horace's praise must be definitive.' We all nodded our heads sagely in agreement. We couldn't think of anything that Horace had said about wine and, at the time, alcohol in any form had not passed our innocent lips; but Falernian sounded splendid stuff.

In another aside full of irrelevant information, our classics master went on to tell us of Galen, the father of modern medicine, who was also physician to the great Stoic Emperor Marcus Aurelius. Poor Marcus had the cares of the world on his shoulders but his stomach constantly let him down. He was a chronic dyspeptic and Galen insisted that he drank copious draughts of Falernian. The master of the world deserved the world's finest wine. To make sure of this, Galen made a personal inspection of the Emperor's vast wine cellar in what must have been the greatest wine binge in ancient history. Such was the quality of the wine, however, that according to his own account at any rate, he emerged without a hangover. After such a recommendation I approached the south Italian wines with eager anticipation. Surely some of the glory of Falernian must have been inherited by a few southern Italian wines at least.

*

I had another reason for hoping for great things from them. This time it was my English master who was responsible. He was none other than Dylan Thomas's father. He took us with loving care through the great masterpieces of English literature, but hesitated a bit as he came to the moderns. Eliot, Auden and his own son, Dylan Thomas, all lay in the future. We stopped with Yeats and the Georgian poets – a whole series of names like Ralph Hodgson, T. Sturge Moore and Wilfrid Wilson Gibson, who seem to have faded from the anthologies beyond recall. Among them was a poet who Dylan's father seems to have met and admired, W. J. Turner, author of a poem entitled 'Talking with Soldiers'. The opening lines powerfully impressed me at the age of seventeen.

> The mind of the people is like mud,
> From which arise strange and beautiful things . . .

There followed a long list of the beautiful things, including

> Mary Magdalena and the vine Lachryma Christi
> Were like ghosts up the ghost of Vesuvius,
> As I sat and drank wine with the soldiers . . .

I didn't know exactly what he meant, but Turner's adding of an 'h' into Lacryma seemed to give the whole thing a romantic charm. You simply had to try a wine with a name like Lacryma Christi, the Tears of Christ. Whatever the contents of their bottles those southern Italians were masters at dreaming up splendid labels. You can picture yourself sampling Lacryma on a sunny patio with a view of Vesuvius and served by a waiter with one of those dazzling smiles that indicates that he could play Verdi on his teeth.

Naturally I made a point of ordering a bottle as soon as I arrived in Naples. Was it the heir to the glories of the old Roman Falernian? Far from it. That formidable late Victorian critic and connoisseur Professor George Saintsbury had harsh things to say about it, in words that would have shaken the modern Italian Tourist Board. He claimed that Lacryma Christi tasted like 'ginger beer, alternately stirred with a stick of chocolate and a sulphur match'. Would any modern wine writer dare to dispel such verbal acid in these mealy-mouthed days? I'm not sure if he was referring to the Rosso, the Bianco or the Rosato, for the wine comes in three varieties and I tried them all. None of them was quite as awful as the bottle described by Saintsbury, but in truth they were no great shakes. My dream of savouring the spirit of the Falernian evoked in the Swansea Grammar School rapidly faded. From the vinous point of view, the sooner the Allies advanced northwards towards Rome and finer wine, the better.

*

But what chance was there of an advance? Snow was falling on the mountains and rain on the rest of southern Italy. This was no time for a *blitzkrieg*. As General Fuller put it, 'Of what use are tanks and aeroplanes and mechanised transport, in a country like this? What you want is an army of bullet-proof kangaroos'.

None of our troops resembled these desirable military marsupials. The only thing we could do was to outflank the Gustav Line by a seaborne landing. So the notorious Anzio Beachhead was born. I attended the briefing at General Mark Clark's headquarters, established in the vast baroque eighteenth-century palace of Caserta outside Naples – 'The only place,' as one British officer put it, 'where you can get your hat blown off indoors.' On the face of it, the plan seemed good. 'Rome in ten days' was the slogan. But our confidence was a little sapped when General Lucas, the American commander in charge of the landing, remarked to his British counterpart, 'This is going to be worse than Gallipoli.' It nearly was, for General Lucas – 'Corn-cob Charlie' to his troops – tried to play safe, never a good plan against the Germans. He had his excuse. General Mark Clark had advised him, 'Don't stick your neck out as I did at Salerno.'

We landed almost unopposed on the night of 22 January 1944. As dawn broke, the unit I accompanied was well out on the road to Rome, and we rounded up a car full of German officers, all as tight as ticks, returning from a dirty weekend in the Italian capital.

We, unfortunately, were in for a far dirtier four months, for the Germans counter-attacked furiously. They nearly pushed us into the sea and we hung on to our few square miles of beachhead by the skin of our teeth. Churchill commented bitterly: 'I thought I had flung a wild cat ashore but all I've got is a stranded whale.' Anzio was a great place for official wisecracks made at a distance and not always appreciated by those of us who were cringing under the shellfire of the beachhead. As one final wisecrack put it, Anzio was 'all hell let loose in a band-box'.

That one sentence is enough. It is just a reminder, as we dwell on the delights of liberation, that we must not forget the agony, the horror, even the nightmare obscenity, of war.

For a wine-lover Anzio had an added misery. When we landed we all assumed that we would drive fast inland to seize the Alban hills. Their graceful outline was clearly visible from the beachhead and we all knew that their slopes were clothed with the celebrated vineyards of the Vini dei Castelli Romani. The experts all told us how superior were their products to the wretched wines we had been swallowing around Naples, but these desirable wines of the Castelli remained mockingly out of our reach. Instead, Field Marshal Kesselring had his headquarters among them, and on the choicest vineyards, the great

long-range gun the troops christened 'Anzio Annie' hurled shells and not vintage bottles at us.

We had to be content with the rough stuff they produced around Anzio and Nettuno. The old medieval township of Nettuno in particular was honeycombed with deep wine cellars, full of the product which the Americans christened 'Dago Red'. These deep cellars were also natural air-raid shelters and at each entrance the notice was placed, *'Al Ricovero'* – 'To the air-raid shelter'. The Americans were no linguists. They thought that Al Ricovero was the name of the wine merchant, and an 'off limit' secret visit to Al's place to purchase huge flasks of Dago Red was a powerful if unofficial morale-builder.

Perhaps liberation was one small and excusable compensation for the boys who had been at the sharp end of the business and survived. This is exactly what we felt when, at long last, we broke out of our Anzio prison. It was the end of May 1944, and ahead of us lay the liberator's dream – Rome, at last!

Rome was the first of the European capitals to be liberated in the Second World War. In the dawning light of 5 June, we entered the outer suburbs. We were not quite certain that we had actually entered the Eternal City, for an American advance unit had removed the 'Roma' roadsign to present it to their commander, General Mark Clark. 'It will look swell on his mantelpiece back home.' Looting or liberation? As the Duke of Wellington said about Waterloo, 'It was a damned near run thing.'

It didn't really matter, for the Romans knew exactly how to deal with an invading army. After all, their city had been liberated more frequently than any other capital in Europe. As a result, the inhabitants had developed the remarkable technique of liberating their liberators. As soon as the Romans realised that the Germans had actually left, they poured into the streets.

Our jeep was engulfed in a cheering crowd and we were fairly hoisted into the nearest café, where we were plied with every liquor under the Italian sun. It was marvellous – until we finally staggered back to the jeep to find that every drop of petrol had been syphoned out of the tank!

After the delirium of the first few days, the Romans settled down happily to the business of gently relieving the unsuspecting GIs of every dollar they possessed. The victims were never aware of the process: they remained under the happy illusion that they were bringing the blessings of freedom to a people long bound in the chains of Fascism. They carried this illusion into the sacred precincts of the Vatican itself. How else can I explain the strange affair of the Holy Father's audience for the press correspondents which took place only a few days after we had entered Rome?

I wish I had sent a report back to the BBC immediately, but, at that moment, Broadcasting House wasn't the remotest bit interested in our goings-on in Italy. The very day after we were being hailed as liberators by the crowds in the streets of Rome, the Allied armies landed on the beaches of Normandy. Overnight we were relegated to the sidelines and, when I remember the events of that strangest of Papal audiences, perhaps it was just as well. It was a classic case of the clash between two cultures, between the New World and the Old.

Our motley group of war correspondents, army film unit cameramen and escorting officers was assembled in the Lesser Throne Room. On the way there one warrior of the typewriter had slipped into the Sistine Chapel and looked up at Michelangelo's 'Eve'. 'Jeze, Thomas,' he shouted at me, 'lamp those Alps. You could tune in to Cincinnati on them.' Not exactly the right mood in which to receive the instructions of a Monsignor who now appeared to inform us of the order of proceedings. Among other information, he told us: 'When the Holy Father comes, he will give you all a pair of beads.' Unfortunately many of the Americans misinterpreted his Irish accent and thought that he had said 'an aperitif'. As the audience progressed there was still a steady murmur in the background, 'Say, when do we get at the hard liquor?'

But now we could almost sense the approach of the Holy

Father coming towards us through those long magnificent corridors, saluted by the Papal Guards in their splendid Raphael-designed costumes. This, we felt, was history in the making. Suddenly, Pope Pius XII stood before us, a white-robed austere figure of innate simplicity and impressive dignity, perfectly framed in the rich Renaissance doorway. A moment to cherish and remember.

Then the dam burst. This was also the moment for which the American photographers had been waiting, and at their head was little Benny Lippman. I had got to know and like Benny at Anzio. He was a New York Jew, brave as a lion, who had carried his camera into the dangers of the front line. He had become a legend on the beachhead, but as he confessed to me afterwards, 'Thomas, I'm not really wised up on this religion stuff. All I know about it is photo-graphing barmitzvahs in Brooklyn before I got drafted.' In a moment, Benny had given the Pope the full barmitzvah treatment. 'OK, boys. Let's go!' – and he led the charge. In seconds the Holy Father was surrounded by a jostling crowd of press photographers, cameras clicking and bulbs flashing. The Monsignori crossed themselves in incredulous horror. When the Imperialists captured Rome in 1527, the Pope hurried to take refuge in the Castel San Angelo. This

19

time there was no escape. The mechanised Goths were already inside the gates.

As the cameras clicked, cameramen hurriedly enquired over their shoulders, 'What do you call this guy, Highness or Holiness?' And even more anxiously, 'Is this guy a family man?' Even photographers have to change films eventually, and as they retired we saw the Pope raise his hand in blessing. Benny wasn't ready but he was determined not to miss his picture. His voice floated through the audience chamber: 'Hold that, Popey. I've got yer outa focus.'

At last, order was restored. We heard the Pope's address and then, with some slight trepidation, he came down the line, followed by a Vatican official carrying a tray of rosaries. His

ordeal wasn't over yet. One American shook the Pope's hand and ordered, 'Photograph me now, Benny. They'll never believe this at Wilkesbarre.' At last the Pope came to me. He enquired anxiously, 'American?' 'No, sir,' I said, 'British.' 'How beautiful,' came his reply. A voice murmured in my ear – again it was the ever present Lippman, ready with the advice, 'Grab two of them rosies, Thomas. With one of them you can lay any Catholic chambermaid in New York.' Thank heavens, I am sure the Pope never heard it and I hope he also missed the sound of the Anzio pipers marching up and down outside in the Piazza San Pietro. With a certain lack of tact, the tune they were playing bore a suspicious resemblance to 'Lilliburlero'!

Disgrace abounding! Diplomatic apologies followed, but I am certain of one thing – the Pope understood and forgave. Of all men, he knew how people behave who have suddenly been released from long strain. It was we who were 'out of focus'.

I had no further time at Rome either for reflection or liberation. The Germans were now pulling back sullenly to the north, where they had already prepared the strong defences of the Gothic Line along the Appennines. I set off to follow them and found our advance units now moving through some of the loveliest scenery in all Italy. The great Florentine painters have immortalised this mellow country of Tuscany, with its roads lined with waving cypresses, neat vineyards ruled along the green slopes, and white villas and churches crowning the hilltops. This was the very same art gallery landscape that Général de Mon̄tsabert was to discuss with me some months later when we were liberating the equally enchanting countryside of Burgundy. I caught up with the French army just out-side the little hill of San Gimignano, north of Sienna.

I also caught up with good Italian wine at last. San Gimignano is on the edge of the Chianti area, and Chianti Classico, when you get hold of a good

21

bottle from a conscientious proprietor, can restore your faith in the Italians as wine producers. I didn't have much time to search out the best, for the French were pushing their advance at a rapid rate through the carefully tended vineyards that surrounded the town. A curious sight, for many of the troops were *goumiers* from North Africa, clad in dark brown hooded robes which gave them a strange resemblance to a band of armed Franciscan friars. I couldn't help savouring the irony of a regiment of Muslims, all pledged by their religion to teetotalism, busy liberating the vineyards which would produce the strong red wine which their religion had forbidden them to taste. The French officers, however, were happy to do all the necessary tasting on behalf of their men.

San Gimignano is a miracle of preservation. The whole place is basically unchanged since the fourteenth and fifteenth centuries. It bristles with tall towers built for protection by the richer families in the Middle Ages; the skyline is Manhattan in miniature, and the churches hold masterpieces of the art of fresco. Clearly, Général de Montsabert had a problem. He carefully looked up in his history books and realised that San Gimignano was high on his own prohibited list. Churches, above all, were sacrosanct. He decided not to send his troops into the town but to outflank it, with the strange sight of his

North African *goumiers*, moving through the vineyards like heavily armed Franciscan monks.

I slipped into the town. The streets were deserted for the Germans didn't abide by the Montsabert code of conduct. They had shelled the town and the streets were littered with broken tiles. There was even a hole or two in the solid medieval towers. I was moving a little apprehensively over the broken tiles when a somewhat portly gentleman leapt out from a nearby doorway. He wore a peaked cap with an inscribed band. He gripped me firmly by the hand. 'Welcome, welcome, signor,' he beamed. 'How glad my heart is at last to see you. I am official guide. I show you everything. Now, follow me. I take you to see all the beautiful *fresci* in all the beautiful

churches and the Palazzo del Populo where the great Dante himself spoke. The collegiate church. Everything. Follow me. Welcome, welcome.'

Once again, as at Rome, the liberator was about to be liberated himself. We approached the collegiate church. My newfound cicerone stood back in long practised admiration.

'Observe the stones. How skilfully carved. *Trecento. E vero!* ' I would have followed his instructions but, at that moment, there was a sharp whistle followed by a loud bang. A shell had landed not many yards down the street. I made a hurried move to the safety of the church. *'Al ricovero, pronto* – to the air-raid shelter, quick,' I hurriedly suggested. My guide was hurt. 'No, no, you have not seen the great "Annunciata" by Ghirlandaio,' he protested, and I had no option but to follow him up a long flight of stairs and stand before the fresco. In other circumstances I would have paid my homage to a glorious painting, but then came another whistle and an even louder bang. Nearer this time. *'Al ricovero,'* I pleaded, but in vain. My guide had got his first Allied tourist, the forerunner of a lucrative flood. He was not going to le me go for a mere shell.

He propelled me up into the great church itself. A vast fresco covered one of the walls and the centre compartment held a Crucifixion, depicted with a stark, compelling power. 'This is by Barna di Siena,' my guide began his patter . . . but before he could continue there was a violent crash and I felt something sting my forehead. I put my hand up and felt blood. I looked across at the fresco: there was now a hole in it. Dust filled the air. I had been hit by a flying fragment of the fresco that depicted the soldiers dicing for the Robe. I looked at the blood on my hand with incredulity. The impossible had happened. I had become the first man to be wounded by an Old Master!

Well, perhaps I should say scratched, for we hurried from

the church and my guide uprooted the local doctor from his shelter who quickly tied up my artistic wound. I wish I had kept the scar. I could have worn it proudly as a unique battle honour. Some years after I met the painter Michael Ayrton, who has made a special study of that Barna fresco. Apparently the artist had created it after he had come through the nightmare of the great plague, the Black Death of 1347. Ayrton christened Barna 'The Terrible Survivor'. I just felt that I had been 'The Lucky Liberator'.

The shelling of San Gimignano set doubts and anxieties racing through my mind – although this had been a comparatively light shell dusting. Modern tourists to San Gimignano will find it hard to believe that it ever took place. Even the damaged Barna frescos have been restored. But we could not take comfort from this at the time, for ahead of us lay Florence, the art capital of Italy and a treasure-house of the world, containing countless masterpieces. What if the full fury of war should fall upon Florence? I felt that I had to be there, even if I would be watching the death agonies of civilisation. After all, when the Day of Judgement arrives and the Last Post is sounded, I bet that there will be a journalist on hand ready to report it. In any case, I was on the verge of my greatest opportunity in my career as a liberator.

I now had to leave the French, whose line of advance would not take them near Florence, and link up again with the British units who were pushing towards the ridges that overlooked the city. I teamed up with another group of correspondents: old friends of mine who had exactly the same feeling: Florence destroyed or Florence saved, in either case – what a story! We were a strangely assorted jeep-load as we drove through the warm Tuscan countryside, chasing the supreme Art Story. There was Eric Linklater: short, slightly balding and with glasses, the last man in the world you would recognise for what he was – a brilliant novelist, a distinguished military historian and a soldier with a heroic record in the First World War. Sy Korman was a US war correspondent, tall, gaunt, raw-boned, his uniform looking as if it had been issued to him by a relief organisation during a famine. He was brave, tireless in pursuit of a story, and the employee of the *Chicago Tribune*. As for myself, I was a red-faced, roly-poly sort of soldier, a fugitive from Falstaff's army.

We came to the high ridges that guard Florence and reported to the HQ of the hospitable 8th Indian Division. Captain Uni Nayar, the Press Officer, did us proud. He produced a curry of epic proportions and we all tucked in; so heartily that when the time came to move, poor Sy Korman had tummy trouble on a big scale.

'Stay where you are,' I reassured him. 'I'll tell you if there's anything happening.' Nayar, Linklater and Querishi, the Reuter's correspondent with the 8th Indians, now joined me in my jeep and we drove north through that landscape of cypress trees, white Renaissance villas and vineyards. The war was erupting over a painting by Fra Filippo Lippi.

The silence of fear held the countryside. The guns thudded here and there and a stray shell whistled overhead on a pointless mission across a powdery-blue sky. On the brow of the ridge before us stood a medieval castle, complete with towers, turrets, battlements and a view towards the distant domes of Florence. We raced up through the dust to avoid giving an easy target to snipers and machine-gunners – for the battle front was all round us and no soldier takes any risks he can conveniently dodge.

We shot into the safety of a small courtyard. Indian soldiers were everywhere, some squatting in the corners, some clapping their hands over the circular *chapattis* that seemed so strange in Renaissance Italy. We had come to the HQ company of the Mahratta Light Infantry. The Colonel was upstairs asleep after dealing all night with a Tiger tank (the heaviest of German tanks) at the bottom of the garden.

Going into the castle, we saw two great golden Crucifixes

leaning against the walls of the entrance, and alongside them a Virgin and Child on a dark wooden panel. 'They are very good,' said Linklater. 'Too good,' said I. 'They must be copies.'

We went into the drawing-room. Cases were stacked against the wall, and a few British soldiers from the signals company attached to the Mahrattas were rummaging among the bookshelves. A pair of invitation cards still lay on the table near the door. I picked up one and read that Lady Ida Sitwell would be at home at Montegufoni and that there would be dancing.

Montegufoni! Of course, this was Sir George Sitwell's castle, with Sitwell books on gardens littered all over the shelves. Everywhere were books, photographs and *objets d'art* which bore the hallmarks of the marvellous and terrifying eccentric who was the father of Osbert, Edith and Sacheverell. Linklater, as a friend of the family, felt he ought to expostulate with the sergeant. 'We were only looking for something like an Agatha Christie,' explained the sergeant, 'but there's damn-all here.'

How wrong he was! At that moment I felt myself being tugged on the arm. I was surrounded by a group of Italian refugees, Papa, Mama and all the *bambinos*. They shouted *'Capolavori del Uffizi. E vero! E vero!'* and propelled me towards the main hall. As they opened the doors I could see stacks of dark frames inside in the gloom. The papa shouted, *'Moment', aspet'.'* He raced around the hall opening the huge shutters. As he opened each shutter shafts of sunlight shot down, like the spots in a theatre, and lit up the frames. Down shot the first shaft and I gave a gasp of delight and astonishment. There before me was one of the world's greatest paintings, Botticelli's 'Primavera'. Down came the second shaft. Again a glorious revelation – Uccello's 'Battle of San Romano'. On through the hall, with shaft after shaft of the sun lighting up picture after picture. Giottos, Cimabues, Andrea del Sartos, Lippis – the greatest concentration of superb paintings I had ever seen. And all at my mercy! For a moment I was overcome with a wild temptation. I could have put an assorted pair of masterpieces in my jeep, whipped them back via the BBC, and spent the rest of my life contemplating my private Botticelli in my study. This could be the triumph of my career as the Great Liberator.

But at that moment a ringing cry of *'Il Professore'* echoed around the hall and my moment of truth ended. Il Professore, one of the librarians of the Uffizi, entered at the run. These were indeed the masterpieces of the gallery. The Allies had bombed the marshalling yards and in panic the Fascists had ordered the paintings to be scattered around Florence. The war rolled north, the Germans had no transport to spare. So there was the anguished Professore bicycling from castle to castle, appealing to unheeding soldiers, on both sides, who had a battle on their hands, to stop shooting for the sake of the Renaissance. He did not get far.

Now at least he had hope. He turned to Linklater. 'You are a colonel. Quickly, you must stop the war.'

We did our best. We roused the CO from his sleep. He'd noticed some paintings about, but he had a Tiger tank to deal with and painting wasn't exactly in his line, although his wife

wasn't bad at water colours. But once we had explained the position, he acted promptly. He cleared out the refugees eating their salami and drinking their Chianti among the Fra Angelicos. Dark Mahratta soldiers stood on guard over the Uccellos. As for the Botticelli – Eric Linklater adjusted his glasses to make sure he had got the right woman, and, on our behalf, imprinted a kiss on the lips of Primavera.

Later, led by the Professore, we ducked and dodged our way along the skyline to the two neighbouring castles of Montaghana and Poppino. The Professore made light of the odd bullets that whistled over. 'I, Cesare Fasola, was an ancient Alpini', and away he bounded with his green pork-pie hat decorated with a small feather.

More paintings – some damaged, some hidden in wine vats for safety which, to the end of time, will exude a slight perfume of Chianti into the exclusive air of art galleries on warm days.

'Now you have seen with your own eyes, you must stop the war.'

We decided that Linklater, as senior man, had more chance of stopping the war than I had. He would stay at divisional HQ; I would race back and send a discreetly worded despatch to the BBC. We pondered carefully on how we would describe Montegufoni so that there would be no danger of bringing down German gunfire on it. 'An old Italian farmhouse' was our best effort. Alas, when they heard it in England, the Sitwells were naturally indignant on hearing the lordly castle on which their family had lavished so much care demoted to a decrepit old farm building, but later Edith Sitwell understandingly forgave me.

Yet perhaps I ought to feel guilt still, for as I picked up the recovered Sy Korman and sped back to the press camp to send off my despatch, a new temptation overwhelmed me. For the first and, as it happened, only time in my life I had a world scoop on my hands. What should a loyal correspondent do? Tell Sy? I just couldn't. When Sy asked me, 'Did you bump into anything interesting up there?' I heard myself replying as from a great distance, 'Not a thing. Everything as quiet as the grave.' Sy, also, has long since forgiven me, but if ever a reporter committed journalistic mayhem, I was that man.

But my words took effect. They were heard back in Rome and the Allied Art Commission hurriedly sent up its experts. Linklater, on his side, had eloquently pleaded the cause of art with the generals, who sealed off this small but precious section of the front. Between us I think we helped to save Primavera and her sisters. But could it be counted as liberation?

When I returned to the Uffizi after the war, Cesare Fasola welcomed me. We walked through the newly hung galleries. Everything was guarded, untouchable, revered. We passed the pictures which I had last seen propped against corridor walls and surrounded by peasant families. Now they seemed to have become impossibly remote again. Then we stood before the 'Primavera'. I remembered how I had touched the painted panel and my surprise at discovering that it was full of tiny worm holes.

Two American ladies stood beside us and looked at the marvellously painted colours, the delicate, heart-moving, fragile beauty of Spring. One turned to the other and said, 'I don't think she looks very healthy, do you?' The other replied, 'I wonder why they make such a fuss about her.'

The Professore and I made no comment. We knew what the

31

fuss was about. We felt that, from now on, we had a secret understanding with Primavera. I was relieved when she came safely through the floods of 1966 that did more damage to Florence in twenty-four hours than the Allies did in four years of war!

Yet the hard fact remains. I had been given the greatest chance in the world to acquire a personal Old Master and I had failed. The lesson was clear. I had set my sights far too high as a fledgling liberator. To operate on the grand scale among the world's masterpieces you must be a Duke of Wellington. Or else a Napoleon, who had kidnapped all those Uffizi paintings and swept them off into the Louvre in Paris 175 years before I arrived at Montegufoni. Great paintings are not legitimate prey for smart twentieth-century operators, for the art experts have carefully listed every one of them. It is only in James Bond fiction that rich and ruthless American tycoons pay for stolen masterpieces.

Yet what about those Old Masters that still decorate the walls of some of our great country houses? How did those British eighteenth-century 'milords' lay their hands on them? Had they already become expert liberators? Yes, for they possessed the greatest of the liberator's assets – they had the cash! There were agents in Italy who specialised in the business of conveying desirable paintings from impoverished Italian noblemen to their well-heeled British counterparts. No problems about export licences in those happy days. But I wonder if the British purchaser got exactly what he paid for. Back in the eighteenth century the Italians had already mastered the complex art of Reverse Liberation.

How many of those dark canvases hanging in many of our stately homes are exactly what they purport to be? I have a suspicion that there was a thriving industry in those days for supplying mass-produced Old Masters at cut prices, and of all shapes and sizes – above all, dark Old Masters whose

authenticity could not be questioned by cleaning. In the eighteenth century in Britain, masterpieces were safer if they remained in the dark. Now where could the centre of conveyor-belt production of masterpieces be found?

I discussed the problem with my old friend Judge Bruce Griffith, art-lover and wit, and he had no hesitation in pinpointing the factory area. 'Look to Venice. It has more dark churches filled with even darker paintings than anywhere else in Italy.' I was a little startled. Ruskin and Turner have created the image of Venice as the City of Light, the nursery of painters like Titian, Tintoretto, Veronese, whose canvases glow with rich colour. But then I remembered how often I had consulted my guidebook to Venice and set off to see a recommended masterpiece in some obscure church. After wandering through a maze of alleys and rickety bridges over slightly smelly side

canals, I would find myself in some baroque structure with the painting hidden in a side chapel lost in ecclesiastical gloom.

Those sixteenth- and seventeenth-century churches are the problem. Art experts may lift their eyebrows, but I maintain that the old Italian Gothic-style churches of the Middle Ages were full of light because the people who built them wanted you to see the frescos on the walls – even if the inspection was attended with danger, as at San Gimignano. But the Renaissance brought a desire to impress, and the church had to be imposing. Columns, classical cornices, colonnades and the rest of the architectural tricks of Imperial Rome. Splendid for exteriors but fraught with difficulties inside. When you are in search of symmetry you are bound to create obscurity in some areas. Yet you still need paintings to fill the corners and the dark parts of the ceilings, even if it is quite difficult to make out what those dark canvases represent. But painting is still expensive. How much money ought you to spend filling dark corners?

It was at this point, Judge Bruce Griffith suggested, that someone must have come forward with a brilliant suggestion. Do you really need masterpieces that could not be seen in the dark? There must have been a family of Dark Corner Masters – the Grittis, starting, perhaps, with Gritti il Vecchio (Anselmo Gritti of Murano). You'll not find him in any of the art books and he would have been more than content to be omitted. Light is the last thing a Dark Corner Master would have

wanted cast on his activities. But I can picture him, a tall, impressive figure with a persuasive tongue, on some sunny sixteenth-century morning calling on the canons of the church of St Jude the Obscure.

'Gentlemen,' I can hear him saying, 'I know that you are planning a complete decorative scheme for your new church and no doubt you've got your eye on that up and coming young chap, Paolo Veronese. He's good, I agree. Damned good, and I'm not saying you shouldn't have him. But he *is* just a trifle expensive. But why not furnish your church on the Gritti plan? Let young Paolo do all the big bits – the high altar, the most important side chapel at eye level. But do you really need such high class stuff for that dark corner under the cornice or over the west window where you can't see anything? Yet you know that you have to have a painting there, so why not put a Gritti on the spot?

'I have got a whole string of picture titles about saints that no one has ever heard of so no one will be anxious to check on them. For that cobwebby corner under the arch supporting the central pillar may I suggest "The Accidental Circumcision of

St John the Contortionist''. For that dark little dome I've got a beautiful "Temptation of St Camphoretta by the Students of the Church of St James the Least of All''. We don't ask for cash down like that fellow Titian used to do. I've got a banker near the Rialto who can arrange for easy payments on the instalment plan every other saint's day. And a final attraction. We paint everything with the patent Gritti pigments, which are guaranteed to darken three times as fast as normal colours. In twenty years I can guarantee that all my paintings will be candle-black – almost invisible. Well, what about it, gentlemen?'

Gritti il Vecchio was the genius who started up the business but there is no doubt that the Gritti method reached its peak under il Vecchio's son, Nicolo, naturally known to his friends as Nitti Gritti. He carried the firm triumphantly through the seventeenth century and his masterpiece of *pintura oscura* is the interior of the Church of Siempre Chiuso, now, unfortunately, hidden behind the extension to the Venetian Cornetto factory. The great period of the Grittis was probably over by the 1720s. The new rococo style was letting too much light into the church and the advent of Tiepolo with his brighter palette destroyed the need for the Gritti technique.

Was the secret of their art completely lost? Not quite. For there came a final period, the Indian summer of the Gritti dynasty. The eighteenth century was the heyday of the Grand

Tour for the wealthy heirs of the British nobility. After they had been carefully led around the cultural sights of Europe – and probably slipped their tutors' surveillance to sample the prohibited delights of Venice – they were expected to bring back some artistic proof of their journey. And who better to supply them with dark old masters than the Grittis? It was the French Revolution and the Napoleonic Wars that destroyed the Grand Tour business and the happy world of the Grittis, but not before they had decorated half the stately homes of Britain.

We owe them a debt of gratitude, and it must be a matter of national concern that there is still no adequate study of the important position of the Grittis in Italian art. We await with deep interest Judge Bruce Griffith's own study, to be published, we understand, under the suggestive title *Lighten Our Darkness*.

An anxious thought now strikes me. If I had eventually yielded to temptation and decided to 'liberate' discreetly one of the less prominent pictures that I had found in the castle of Montegufoni, it would have been just my luck to have picked on the only Gritti that had somehow sneaked into the Uffizi!

I had no further opportunity to contemplate the liberation of art. I was hurriedly recalled to Rome and left to others the bringing of freedom to Florence. I was now launched on a far more promising scheme of liberation: the South of France Landing. I could not help thinking, as I studied the plan, that it was easier to carry away a bottle of wine than a fine painting.

But what exactly was the plan? Let us now end our long excursion on the Italian scene and return to Provence, to that café behind St Tropez where the Colonel and I were sitting in the warm sun, enjoying our first bottle of French wine after a landing that had been delightfully easy – all cheering and processions through olive groves. We were savouring the first pleasures of liberation, but already certain spoilsport military critics were questioning our right to be in the south of France at all. Our operation had been grandiloquently christened 'Anvil', but these sour experts claimed that our anvil had nothing to strike on. The Germans, after all, were quietly melting away to the north of their own free will!

Perhaps, after the long passage of the years, we need reminding that this all took place two months after the D-Day landings in Normandy. The Americans under General Patch and the French under Général de Lattre de Tassigny landed on the Riviera and swept up the Rhône valley to link up with General Eisenhower's armies advancing across northern France. 'Vital to the task of smashing the Germans before they reached the Rhine,' insisted Eisenhower. 'Fatal to our hopes of forestalling the Russians in the Balkans,' lamented Churchill.

But time softens controversy and the history of distant wars grows mellow like '53 burgundy. At last we can see Anvil in its true perspective. It was not fought for military motives at all. One glance at the map and the routes taken by the invading armies makes the *raison d'être* of the Anvil campaign crystal clear. It was designed to save some of the greatest vineyards of France.

Was it possible, with the German front starting to crumble elsewhere, that these national treasures should be left at the mercy of the Nazis, especially with the vintage only a few months ahead? General Eisenhower and Sir Winston Churchill may not quite have appreciated the urgency of the situation, but there was one man who did. Général de Monsabert was one of the most trusted generals of the new French army. He was a soldier of energy and resource but, more important for the future of France and for our own cellars, he was a lover of wine. He was at the centre of the planning of Anvil. I need say no more.

I admit that I have no documentary evidence that the gastronomic Général played the decisive role in swinging the invasion towards the threatened vineyards, but historians cling too readily to official documents. I prefer to trust the subtle hints that the Général himself gave me when the campaign was safely over and we were enjoying the hospitality of the wine-growers of Nuits-Saint-Georges.

We were pouring out bottles of such quality that the Général's usual sense of security became slightly less strict than usual. We fought all over again the campaigns we had shared together and I broached the vital question, 'Why did we have to land in France? Would it not have been better to continue up Italy in full strength and with the Germans on the run?'

'My friend,' said the Général, 'you do not consider sufficiently one great difficulty. In Italy, we were fighting our way not through a country but through an art gallery and a museum. It was no longer the Art of War but the War of Art. How could we deploy our full strength? The fifteenth century? I could not attack but had to make an outflanking movement. The sixteenth? Then I permitted myself a little machine-gun fire. The seventeenth? Ah! now we could have artillery support. The eighteenth meant tanks and for the nineteenth, monsieur, I had no hesitation in calling in the air. If only Italy had all been built in the twentieth century we should be on the Alps by now!'

'And Anvil?'

'Let us rechristen it "Winepress". I admit the idea commanded my immediate support. In Italy, all we could do was smash things and the world does not like to hear of works of art being smashed, even in the best of causes. But in this campaign, we come as saviours of the greatest works of art in the world!'

'Works of art, mon général?'

'But certainly – the vineyards of Burgundy.'

So it was that the Anvil campaign combined glory and pleasure in a way never achieved before or since in modern war. In the actual plan of the advance, I detected the subtle thinking of a man of wine. Take, for instance, the lines of attack assigned to the different commands. The American army swung due north from the Riviera through the rough country of the Basses-Alpes, with the task of cutting in on the Germans who were retreating up the actual valley of the Rhône. Their job was vital and took them through superb, high and rough country, but the vinously minded historian will note that it did not take them near a single vineyard of quality.

Now follow the line of advance planned for the French. The soldiers of Général de Lattre de Tassigny and Général de

Montsabert would follow the valley and west bank of the Rhône. Before them lay a succession of mouth-watering names, from Châteauneuf-du-Pape to Mâcon, a glorious symphony of popping corks even before Burgundy came into range. The Germans were pulling out rapidly and holding off our advance units with quick rearguard actions. The French, from their side, and the Americans from theirs, were also trying to outrun the Germans in the hope of getting ahead and then cutting in across the line of the German retreat. All this presented the French command with a serious problem. How could they maintain the momentum of their advance and yet do justice to the great cellars that lay ahead?

It was here that I realised that I could offer our gallant allies an essential service. While they chased the flying enemy, I could pause for a moment to reassure the wine producers that freedom really had arrived.

It was time that the Colonel and I rose while we could from our café chairs and followed the advance. Our first stern duty, after all, was to report the arrival of freedom to Provence.

CHAPTER TWO

An Innocent in the Wine World

Provence, that magical countryside perpetually bathed in the bright light of canvases of Van Gogh and Cézanne: Provence, mirrored in the music of Bizet's 'L'Arlésienne', and where they still danced *Sur le Pont d'Avignon*; Roman Provence of the great amphitheatres of Arles and Orange and the magnificent arches of the Pont du Gard; smiling, seductive Provence of Alphonse Daudet's *Lettres de mon moulin* – yea, I had landed on the beach at St Tropez with my mind as full of romantic images of Provence as the most over-written tourist brochure. 15 August was my birthday and once I had drunk that welcoming champagne and realised that I was safe and alive, I felt that the whole countryside had been presented to me as a birthday gift. Above all, I anticipated the delights of the wines of Provence, for ever since Keats's 'Ode to a Nightingale' had been drilled into me at school, his lines about Provençal vintages had irresistible charm. They even ran in my mind as I crouched in that LST before the ramp went down.

> O, for a draught of vintage! that hath been
> Cool'd a long age in the deep-delved earth,
> Tasting of Flora and the country green,
> Dance, and Provençal song, and sunburnt mirth!

The bit about sunburnt mirth was especially attractive. A wine must have special powers if it can produce all that in a consumer, with dance and Provençal song thrown in. When the Colonel and I sat down to that liberated bottle in the little café behind St Tropez, I almost expected to see a quotation from Keats on the label.

As for judging the wine, however, that notorious 'environment factor' came into play. How could you criticise a bottle which has been presented to you free on a gloriously sunlit morning when you find yourself surrounded by excited Frenchmen slapping you on the back and pretty French girls queuing up to kiss you? I was back in the Budapest situation and this bottle seemed to have the same glorious taste as the Lake Balaton wine I had drunk before the war.

I became more composed, more ready to make a judgement on Provençal wines in the days that followed. The main body of the German army was pulling out rapidly from Provence and making for the valley of the Rhône, but the enemy command had left 'do-or-die' units in the docks of Toulon and Marseilles to try and deny us their use as long as possible. So I found myself, in the days that followed the landing, covering the French army's mopping-up operations along the coast. In the process we reached that remarkable area to the east of Marseilles they call the Calanques – full of minor fiords cut into gleaming limestone cliffs. I was driving my jeep with care down one of these minor canyons towards what looked like a little restaurant on the sea's edge when, for the second time, I was hailed by an unmistakable British voice. By heavens, it was the Colonel. 'Haven't been able to meet anyone yet among the Froggies who speaks English,' he explained, 'so thought I'd follow the front and see the fun.'

'I think there's plenty of fun straight ahead over the hill,' I

said rather nervously. 'There are still Germans about some-where.' A recent tank track led down towards the restaurant. The Colonel leapt out and bent down with his hand on the track. With all the experience of an old tiger-hunting *shikari*, he immediately pronounced, 'Spoor's hot. It's one of ours.'

Safe in the knowledge that there were no Germans left around, we went down to the little restaurant. Again we had the luck of the liberator. The proprietor had just returned and was ready to serve his first customers. We sat on the verandah overlooking the bright sea. He produced a bottle of red wine and rushed backstage to prepare the meal. Here, surely, was my opportunity to give a fair judgement on Provençal wine, to see if it lived up to Keats's poetic praise. It was a red wine from the vineyards of Bandol through which we had already driven. Was it about to justify those singing lines of Adonais? The Colonel simply walloped his glass down – long residence in India and a devotion to hot curry are not conducive to the cultivation of a sensitive palate. I lifted my glass to my lips and I must admit that I felt a sharp sense of disappointment. It wasn't so much that the wine was bad, it was quite reasonable in its way, a good *vin ordinaire*, but by no stretch of the imagination did it live up to the poet's advertisement. Where was that 'taste of Flora' that he had promised me? Come to think of it, what on earth did he mean by a taste of Flora?

Let us examine the rest of the verse that follows those thrilling first four lines:

O for a beaker full of the warm South
Full of the true, the blushful Hippocrene,
With beaded bubbles winking at the brim
And purple-stained mouth;
That I might drink, and leave this world unseen,
And with thee fade away into the forest dim.

The mystery increases. That reference to Hippocrene, for example. The Hippocrene spring rose on Mount Helicon, and was the source of poetic inspiration to the Ancient Greeks. Keats was no teetotaller and was certainly not thinking of water to inspire his muse. He was surely justified in using poetic licence to maintain that the 'true' Hippocrene was wine. But what sort of wine? He lists a remarkable collection of qualities, but could they all be united in one bottle and could that bottle have come from Provence? It was obviously young, for it gave you a 'purple-stained mouth'. I looked across at the Colonel and there was no purple tinge on his crisp moustache. But then he had gulped his wine down and no staining drop would have had the remotest chance of touching his lips. Then there is the curious business of those 'beaded bubbles winking at the brim'. As far as I could discover there were no sparkling Provençal wines or even some *pétillant* ones. And a final puzzle. Keats describes this remarkable vintage – a red wine – as being served ice-cold. None of this tricky business of the wine being *chambré* for him!

Many years later I came across a possible solution to the Nightingale Mystery. Marghanita Laski, in a most ingenious and well-researched article in that delicious vinous entertainment entitled *The Compleat Imbiber* with which Cyril Ray used to enchant all conscientious wine-lovers in the years just after the war, had investigated Keats's drinking habits. She was convinced that the wine he had in mind never came from Provence but was a claret. Keats's letters are full of praise for claret. He proclaimed, 'Give me Books, fruit, French wine and fine weather and a little music out of doors, and I could pass a summer very quietly.' Yes, a recipe for tranquil happiness that we could all enjoy.

But then Marghanita Laski went on to prove that poor Keats may have thought that he was drinking claret, but that it most certainly wasn't Latour or Lafite or even a wine from Bordeaux. The word 'claret' covered a multitude of vinous sins in those days. Keats and his friends were poor men. Their claret that they thought came from France was probably a vinho verde from Portugal, which was certainly young, purple and *pétillant*. Its importation had not been interrupted by the Napoleonic wars and it had probably cornered the market for cheap claret.

A sad story. If ever a poet deserved a Latour or even my '53 la Tâche it was John Keats! But I console myself with the thought that, as he sat listening to the nightingale in that Hampstead garden, he wasn't drinking that somewhat nondescript stuff with which the Colonel and I were washing away the memory of that unhappy horse. In truth, the wines of this part of lower Provence are no great shakes.

We gulped down our last glass and looked out over that calm sea shining in the sun. How quiet it all was! Over the hills behind us our tanks were reaching the outskirts of Marseilles. It was time to go back to the war. There were handshakes and warm thanks all round. 'You must come back,' beamed our host. 'Freedom has arrived and we will celebrate again. You must come back and drink a bottle again of this excellent wine.' 'Not with horse-meat, I hope,' muttered the Colonel; 'And not this particular wine,' I also murmured under my breath. Of course, I never expected to see that little café or that lonely limestone gulf again. We, the liberators, had paused at so many similar places, to enjoy a moment's delight and then pass on never to return.

By a strange twist of fate, fifteen years to the very day I had first come to that café, I found myself sitting at the self same spot,

drinking the same wine – no, it didn't seem to have improved – and looking out over the same bright sea. Only this time I wasn't going to merely contemplate the sea, I was going to dive under it.

My instructor was none other than Captain Jacques Cousteau himself. The BBC were co-operating with French television to transmit the first underwater pictures ever seen on the TV screen. Captain Cousteau had discovered a Greek galley, which had been sunk off this coast nearly two thousand years before. It had been full of wine amphorae and we proposed to lift them to the surface in full view of the television audience.

It was a daring project for the time, for as yet we had no method of pre-recording on tape. Everything had to go out live, and this gave a special 'kick' to the programme, as did the behaviour of certain of the French *techniciens*. Radio-Télévision

Française, the French BBC, at that moment was going through one of its complicated administrative reconstructions which had earned it the secondary title of Radio-Confusion Française. As I sat in the café and looked across to Cousteau's *Calypso* anchored in the bay, I sensed that there was some tension between the man who was going to direct the programme and some of his engineers who were going to dive. No amount of that Provençal wine seemed to close the gap between them.

I must say, however, that out of apparent confusion the *techniciens* were now bringing about order – no doubt employing the celebrated French 'System D', the slang term for the great French gift of improvisation. They dropped cameras into the water and swung heavy equipment up the cliffs. Everything they did defied the practices of the BBC, and even the basic laws of electrical engineering, but somehow everything worked.

The opening shot of the programme for French viewers was designed to show the first amphora being sent to the surface from the wrecked galley by the ingenious method of filling it with compressed air. The director bellowed his orders to his *techniciens* far below and my French counterpart announced, with some flamboyance, 'Messieurs, mesdames. The magic moment has arrived. For the first time, the treasures of the past now come to the surface after being hidden in the depths of the sea for nearly two thousand long years.' This was also the magic moment of revenge for which the *techniciens* too had been waiting. They had taken down into the depths a box of those tactful accessories the French know as *capotes anglaises*. These were quietly filled with compressed air and then sent shooting up to the surface. The treasures of the deep now offered to the astonished French viewers gave only too convincing evidence that the French people were world leaders in birth control! All this took place, of course, in the Dark Ages before the Pill. But, then, who can foretell the future?

*

I got a surprising answer to that somewhat rhetorical question after the delirium of the liberation of Marseilles. We caught up, once again, with the advance units as they entered the town of Salon. Once again, the crowds poured into the streets, the flags erupted from every window, the *collaborateurs* made themselves scarce and the unfortunate ladies who had consorted with the Germans had their heads shaved. We were plied with Provençal wine and treated as if we were the personal delegates sent by Winston Churchill to the Mayor of Salon.

Salon, however, offered us a journalistic problem. How did the bringing of freedom to this somewhat nondescript Provençal town rate in the merit table of war reporting? Unfortunately, not very highly. Would any editor worth his salt throw aside a vivid despatch from Chester Wilmot with Monty's army racing across the Seine towards Brussels in favour of an account by me of the now standardised goings-on in the streets of Salon? The plain answer was a resounding 'No'. Yet I felt that I had to send back some sort of despatch. An editor far from the scene of action gets deeply suspicious if silence falls on a correspondent for any length of time. He starts checking up on how much it costs to keep his man in a spot where nothing seems to be happening. The next time the correspondent forwards his expenses he may get one of those classic telegrams that the brilliant reporter the late René Cutforth received when, at long last, he submitted his expenses from Korea. Said the telegram: 'Please note that we have sent you to report the Korean war and not to finance it.'

In this situation, the best trick is to forget all about direct reporting from the front and look around for what used to be called a 'human story'. I had already planned my human story for the liberation of Avignon which now lay ahead of Salon. I would get the local schoolchildren to assemble on the bridge and sing *'Sur le Pont d'Avignon'*. At this distance of time, such a story looks too 'ham' to credit. But the obvious may sometimes be a winner. This one went down a treat. The editors found a place for it, even when we were about to enter Brussels. But what on earth could poor Salon supply in the human interest line?

The guide book was no help. It stated, with blunt honesty, *'Salon n'a pas de ces grandes curiosités qui attirent et retiennent l'automobiliste de passage.'* In other words, 'If you've got a car, carry on and don't bother to stop here unless you have to!' I was rescued from my dilemma by Jacques, a quietly spoken middle-aged man who turned out to be a local schoolmaster. To my cry of despair, 'Did anything ever happen in Salon?' he replied with some pride, 'But of course, this was the home of the great Nostradamus. He's buried in l'Église St Laurent. He is our great man. You should pay tribute to him.'

Nostradamus! Yes, here was something definitely 'off-beat' which, after all, might yet make a news item out of Salon. Michael Nostradamus was the remarkable Renaissance physician, seer and prophet who had been born at St Rémy in Provence but who had eventually settled down in Salon, having travelled constantly throughout France acquiring a great reputation in court circles. He was especially patronised by Catherine de Medici and published a celebrated treatise on perfumes and face-lotions. It is important to remember that he was no charlatan but a highly respected doctor who had shown his courage and skill by battling successfully with the terrible plague that had decimated Aix. But he obtained a European reputation when, in 1555, he published his book of prophecies now called the *Centuries*. It became a best seller overnight.

At first sight, nothing looks further removed from the best seller list than the *Centuries*. The book consists of a long string of quatrains written in crabbed verse and linked together by no obvious theme. In his preface, Nostradamus admits that he has written his prophesies in 'abstruse and twisted sentences'. That's putting it mildly. The quatrains defy all the laws of syntax, verse and intelligibility. There may have been a good reason for this deliberate obscurity, however. Nostradamus came from a Jewish family which had been converted to Christianity, but no doubt the Inquisition still kept its eye on him. Looking into the future could be a dangerous business in the sixteenth century, hence the contorted verses and the deliberately obscure allusions. But perhaps it is this very obscurity that irresistibly attracts men of a certain mental stamp – the same sort of people who used to solve those fiendish old Torquemada crosswords in *The Times*. All through the long years after 1555 there have been Nostradamus fans busy worrying away at every verse in the *Centuries*, and my Salon schoolmaster was such a Nostradamus worrier. I have a feeling that his friends had long since given up listening to him on his favourite subject. You can hear them whispering: 'For God's sake don't start old Jacques Ducros off on Nostradamus or we'll be here all night!' But at last he had a chance of finding a sympathetic listener. He dashed back home to get his copy of the *Centuries* and soon we were seated at the inevitable café with the inevitable bottle of Provençal wine and Jacques in full enthusiastic flight.

I must admit that the more I listened to Jacques giving his interpretation of those rugged quatrains the more I became convinced that there was something in old Nostradamus after all. What was the moment Nostradamus called the '*commun achèvement*' – the 'vulgar advent' – but the coming of the French Revolution? Nostradamus, in one of his prefaces, even gives a precise date for the final spoilation of the French Church in the Revolution – 1793. Jacques kept on producing verses that seemed to refer conclusively to the imprisonment of the King and his family in the Temple. Then, in triumph, he quoted a quatrain which he obviously regarded as the clincher, the most clear-cut proof yet that Nostradamus knew of the French Revolution in astonishing detail 234 years before it actually happened.

In 1791, the King decided to escape from the Tuileries in Paris and make his way secretly to the eastern frontier where he knew he had troops waiting who would support him against the revolutionaries. The incident is known to history as the Flight to Varennes. The whole adventure was badly mismanaged. Louis was dressed in grey so as not to be conspicuous but the Queen wore white. The royal family were recognised and intercepted at Varennes, an obscure little town in Lorraine which has never entered history before or since. Incredible as it may seem, Varennes appears in this quatrain by Nostradamus:

> *De nuict viendra par la forest de Reines*
> *Deux pars, vaul torte, Herne, la pierre blanche,*
> *Le moyne noir en gris dedans Varennes:*
> *Elue Cap. Cause tempeste, feu, sang, tranche.*

'What about that last line?' demanded Jacques, ' "The Elected Capet"? By 1781 Louis had become a constitutional monarch. And *tranche* – surely the Guillotine!'

After the war, I met the late James Laver of the Victoria and Albert Museum and a serious student of Nostradamus lore. He supplied additional interpretations of the rest of the stanza. For the first two lines he suggested, 'By night will come through the forest of Reines two married people by a round-about way' – *vaul* is valley and *torte* is twisted. But what about Herne? This could be an anagram for *reine*, queen. Apparently the rules of anagram-making in the sixteenth century allowed for the suppression or substitution of one letter. And the same would go for *noir* in line three. This could be an anagram of *roi*, making Louis the 'Monk King'. A good description for poor Louis, maintained Mr Laver, for it is common knowledge that, as a young man, he was impotent for the first years of his marriage to the fascinating Marie Antoinette. And what was the 'white stone' in line two? Perhaps a reference to the Affair of the Diamond Necklace which did so much to make the Queen so profoundly unpopular?

All very ingenious, but it's still the last line and the single word 'Varennes' that carries conviction. The Elected Capet and his family were brought back to Paris to a furious political storm which ended in blood, fire and the Guillotine. By this time, as you can see, Jacques had me in his spell as firmly as the Ancient Mariner had held the Wedding Guest. He pronounced verse after verse which forecast the triumphs of Napoleon, the Franco-Prussian War and even the First World War, but now I was urging him on. What about our own time? Did old Nostradamus forecast the advent of Hitler? If so, was there a verse which forecast exactly how and when the war would end? I was already framing a lighthearted, witty piece: it would not make the main news but there were plenty of magazine producers who would be happy to find a place for it, and at least it would prove that I was hard at work for the glory of the BBC.

Jacques had no difficulty at all in conjuring up Hitler. What about this?

> *Bestes farouches de faim fleuves trainer,*
> *Plus part du champs encore Hister sera,*
> *En cage de fer le grand fera trainer*
> *Quand rein enfants de German observera.*

This can be translated, if you have the confidence of faith, as: 'Beasts mad with hunger will make the rivers tremble. More and more land will Hister conquer. The great ones will be dragged in an iron cage. The children of the Germans will observe [or, perhaps, respect] nothing.'

Yes, Hister does seem extraordinarily close to Hitler. Not quite as close as Varennes, maybe, but still close enough to send the imagination soaring. You could certainly call the Nazis 'beasts mad with hunger' for world domination, driving their armies across the trembling rivers of northern France in a triumphant *blitzkrieg*. And these 'sons of Germany' observed no moral restraint at all.

Old Nostradamus had clearly shaken me with his Hister – Hitler combination. Now only one thing remained to clinch the conversion: a verse accurately predicting the fate of Hitler and the way in which and the time when the war would end. Feverishly Jacques searched the obscure pages. There were all sorts of references to future disasters yet that final certainty eluded us. Jacques grew desperate and declared, 'I am in touch with an important circle of Nostradaman students in Paris. They will already have found the solution. I will write to them and you will wait for a few days at Salon. Think of the glory to you if they convince you – and the glory, too, for our dear town of Salon.'

Unfortunately, I could not wait for the answer from Paris – not even for the glory of Nostradamus and his dear old town of Salon. The war was hurrying on northwards towards Avignon, and the further north I went, the quicker the aura of old Nostradamus seemed to fade. It has always been the same with me. I am a believer when I am in the Presence, and a Doubting Thomas as soon as I am by myself again. The paranormal, the occult, ghosts and ghost-hunting – I have had occasion, during my broadcasting career, to look at them all, and while I am looking I tremble on the verge of belief. Yet, somehow, I always draw back. I think I must have an inbuilt incredulity, a throwback to my rationalistic upbringing. As a Celt I am supposed to be 'fey', extra-sensitive to the mysterious and the occult, but some very prosaic Druid must have presided over my birth. How else could I have failed to secure the greatest prize ever offered to a paranormal investigator – the first broadcast of a genuine, guaranteed poltergeist!

It happened only a few years after my non-starter with Nostradamus. The war had ended without waiting for Nostradamus's instructions and I was back with the BBC's Outside Broadcasts department in London, helping to re-start peacetime broadcasting. The inventive head of OBs was searching for new sensations for the listeners to replace the heady excitements of the war. Why not broadcast a poltergeist? – if only we could catch one of these mysterious beings at his nefarious work of hurling the furniture all over the place. It was the BBC's search for a plausible poltergeist that brought me in touch with that prince of ghost-hunters, the late Harry Price.

Harry was the most famous psychic investigator in the years between the wars. I am not certain if, by now, Harry quite knew in what world he was living, and after a few weeks of investigation with Harry, I wasn't sure either. He had irresistible charm, however, and convinced the BBC that he could supply them with their much sought-after poltergeist.

Then began a series of adventurous evenings, when Harry's voice would reach me in my office just as the long day's routine was beginning to pall. 'My dear chap, this time I've got an absolute winner. Meet me at the Reform at 6.30, and prepare for an impressive night.' I would find him sitting in that vast hall of the Reform Club in Pall Mall with its air of still waiting for the return of Phineas Fogg after his race around the Victorian world in eighty days. 'Have some port,' Harry would insist, 'the club still has a few bearable bottles left.' To this day I associate my adventures with Harry Price with the Taylor's '27, but any fine old port will send my mind back to those evenings in 1946 when the BBC car would carry us through the still darkened London streets to some semi-detached villa in the outer suburbs where a sure-fire poltergeist had taken up residence. Just as Sherlock Holmes lured the stolid Dr Watson to high adventure in Tooting Bec and Upper Norwood, so

Harry Price cast an air of mystery for me over the dull uniformity of suburbia. But somehow or other, once I had arrived at, for example, 'Dunromin' in Golders Green, or No. 91 Windsor Terrace, Mitcham, those ornaments which I had been assured had been leaping wildly off the mantelpiece the night before all stayed firmly in place. Once again, I seemed to be acting as a psychic repellant!

At last there came one evening when Harry was absolutely positive he had a poltergeist which would even convince the BBC, and once again, like Holmes and Watson, we set off through the semi-darkness of post-war London to investigate Harry's latest case. As we drove, probably inspired by the Reform Club's vintage port, I couldn't help musing on the drinking habits of the famous pair. Holmes was obviously a wine lover but I'd always pictured the stolid Dr Watson as a confirmed beer man. Not so. The old Doctor had hidden depths and surprising tastes. In the 'Sign of Four', for example, Watson, who has only recently taken up residence with Holmes in their famous 'pad' at 221a Baker Street, plucks up courage to tackle his formidable co-lodger on his habit of taking drugs. Watson attributes his courage to the Beaune he had taken for lunch. I wonder what sort of Beaune it was, for Watson had spent a lot of time on the North-west Frontier of India, and I therefore assumed that he had a palate like the Colonel's. Nevertheless, we must welcome old Watson to the ranks of wine drinkers.

Holmes was another matter. He clearly knew his wines and applied his keen, analytical mind to their appreciation. Unfortunately, among his many monographs which include the celebrated treatise 'On the Distinction between the Ashes of Various Tobaccos', we have nothing from the Master on wine. On Watson's evidence we know that Holmes had a pretty taste in vintage port. He ordered a bumper of it to entertain Watson and the Scotland Yard detective Athelney Jones and calm their nerves as they were about to embark on a dangerous chase down the river. It must have been remarkable stuff for, according to Watson, Holmes's conversation had never been more brilliant. 'He spoke on a quick succession of subjects – on miracle plays, on medieval pottery, on Stradivarius violins, on the Buddhists of Ceylon and on the warship of the future!' No wonder poor Athelney Jones sat back open-mouthed. After that cascade of information it was a wonder that he could concentrate at all on catching the criminal.

Holmes applied his wine knowledge to the solving of many of his cases. Keen fans will remember his brilliant solution to the sinister affair at the Abbey Grange where Sir Eustace Brackenstall had been found foully murdered in his own dining-room. An empty bottle of port stood nearby on the table along with three glasses, all of which looked as if they had been used. One contained 'bees-wing', the thick deposit thrown by a bottle of good vintage port. Holmes immediately deduced that only two not three people had drunk from the bottle and that they had poured some wine into the third glass to throw everyone (but Holmes) off the scent.

I could have done with Holmes – port and all – when we came at last to Price's most puzzling case. It concerned a haunted vicarage in the Home Counties – right out of a story by Edgar

Allan Poe, surrounded by dark yews and overlooking a grave-
yard. The owls hooted as the vicar met us at the churchyard
entrance. Price adopted his best bedside manner. 'Now, my
dear sir, what exactly is worrying you?' The vicar looked a
little doubtfully at me. Harry reassured him. 'You may speak
freely in front of Mr Vaughan-Thomas. He is a most exper-
ienced investigator.'

'Well', said the vicar. 'The phenomenon seems to occur in
the evening around the time I am preparing to go to bed.'

'Ah, yes,' Harry agreed, 'typical of poltergeist phenomena.
Typical.'

'I feel a sort of column of cold air approaching me.'

'Yes, indeed. A typical poltergeist phenomenon.'

'It seems to encircle me.'

'Typical, typical,' said Harry.

'Then when I bend down to say my prayers ... I find it a little difficult to explain.'

'Speak freely, my dear sir, speak freely.'

'Well the ... I feel I am being violently interfered with ... from behind.'

'Ah yes,' said Harry. 'Typical poltergeist ...' and then he stopped in his tracks. Typical? Far from it. We were in the presence of the first  queer poltergeist in the history of psychic research.

We retired to keep watch in the room next to the vicar's. 'We will be on the watch,' Harry assured the vicar. 'As soon as you feel the cold air, thump with your stick and we'll be with you like a shot.'

'I'll take the first watch,' said Harry, and I composed myself to sleep. Suddenly I awoke to find light streaming in through the window and Harry gently snoring at my side. I shook him quickly and he gasped, 'Good God. The vicar!' We rushed into the next room, falling over a trip wire on the way. The vicar was sitting up in bed. He regarded us reproachfully. 'I gave you the signal but no one came.' And then he added, more in sorrow than in anger, 'The phenomenon occurred three times during the night.'

We had no option but to pack our Gladstone bags and retire. I had found our poltergeist but dared not put him on the air. This was still the non-permissive world as far as homo-sexuals were concerned. I could not be a pioneer of Gay Lib in the realm of the occult. Let us return to reality and our advance through the smiling land of liberated Provence on those sunny days of August 1944, when there were no ghosts on the horizon – only the hard excitement of pursuing the fleeing Germans toward the entrance of the valley of the Rhône.

CHAPTER THREE

Return to
the Vine

I fear I have dismissed the world of ghosts too soon from this history of the Liberation of Burgundy. No sooner had I left Salon and abandoned Nostradamus as an advisor on strategy than I found myself, with a French advanced unit, approaching France's one authentic ghost-town. Les Baux is perched on a rocky spur of the Alpilles, those little forerunners of the Alps that suddenly shoot out of the flat, fertile Provençal plain. Our scout car swung off the main road with the object of getting on to the high ground from which we could see if the Germans had left any strong rear guards behind them. Suddenly we found ourselves in a moon landscape of jagged rocks, as if the Egyptian desert of the Valley of the Kings had been transported to France. Grotesque teeth of limestone thrust themselves out of the ground, fretted into impossible shapes until you protested that what this landscape needed was not a painter but a good dentist. Perched on the highest group of rocks, which broadened on the southern side into a little plateau cut off by precipices, was a ruined town, a chaos of crumbling walls, empty windows and narrow, silent lanes that climbed higher and higher among the yellowing rocks until, at last, they brought you out at the summit château, with the whole vast

plain of the lower Rhône below you – olive groves, rice fields, the wide glittering lakes of the Carmargue.

The French officer with me climbed on to the top of the ruins and scanned the landscape with his field glasses. Occasionally a little puff of smoke shot up among the olive groves below and we heard the rattle of machine guns. The officer shut his glasses with a snap. 'They're pulling out. They are just firing to keep our heads down. They'll be gone by the afternoon. We've time for a good lunch. Follow me.'

When it comes to liberation in their own country, the officers of the French army are clearly supreme. Up until now, the Colonel and I had, as it were, stumbled on hospitality and we had been celebrating freedom with what was, to be honest, glorified 'plonk'. This French officer knew exactly where to find the best in wine and cookery. Up in Les Baux lay the Hôtel Beaumanoir, then one of the greatest restaurants in the south

of France. It was tucked away among the rocks with a great view from the terrace. 'They will be glad to see us,' said the officer significantly, and indeed they were. Just as Drake declared, when they told him that the Armada was in sight as he was playing bowls on Plymouth Hoe, 'We have time to finish the game and beat the Spaniards too', so my companion decided, 'We will have time for an excellent lunch and then we will see off those troublesome German gentlemen below. But first, a good bottle!'

So we sat in the warm sun, alone on the *terrace*, the most privileged tourists in France, with a noble cellar at our command and drinking our first glasses of wine as the chef began his labours off-stage for our delight. My officer turned out to be the son of a wine merchant in Lyon and was looking forward eagerly not only to a family reunion but to being the first to liberate all the most famous vineyards of the Rhône valley. They now lay ahead of us in all their glory, a splendid curtain-raiser for the even greater wines of Burgundy. What a roll-call! Châteauneuf-du-Pape, Tavel which produces the best *vin rosé* in France; Tain l'Hermitage where the wines once rivalled the greats in Bordeaux until they were ruined by phylloxera; the wines of the Côte Rôtie, a string of splendours including the white wine we were now drinking, the rare Château-Grillet. It had, I thought, almost a hock-like flavour and utterly unlike any wine I had previously drunk. My companion gave me a run-down on the Rhône wines as we waited for the *bonne bouche* which was to go with the Grillet – as I remember, a delicious dish of crawfish tails. He was clearly an enthusiast for the wines of the Rhône. In fact, he launched off into the whole saga of wine-growing in the region, particularly of Châteauneuf-du-Pape. 'Ah, the oldest wine in France, for some say that the vines were brought here by the Greeks in 600 BC. Or perhaps they came back with the Crusaders. In any case they are splendid. Our Rhône wines can hold up their heads with the best of them. They are strong, masculine – wines for real men!'

As I drank and listened a great doubt started to possess me, a modest anxiety. As I listened to all this expertise, I began to wonder if I was really prepared for the great task that lay ahead. Would I be the right man in the right place when it came to the Liberation of Burgundy? Perhaps the time has now come – as I remember how we sat in the sunlight of Les Baux drinking Château-Grillet – to look back on my wine-drinking career before I landed in the south of France, my boozing autobiography, as it were, my vinous confessions from the first days when I lifted a wine-glass to my lips.

I suppose I ought to be surprised that I ever became a wine drinker for I come of a race, the Welsh, who are not supposed to be fervently attached to the product of the grape. When I was growing up – more years ago than I care to remember but I'll admit it was before the First not the Second World War – Welsh society was strongly Nonconformist. By the middle of Victoria's reign, the chapel had finally triumphed over the church. Bethels, Bethanias, Hermons and Bethesdas littered the landscape and every one was a stronghold of teetotalism.

The supporters of drink – the English-speaking landlords and the wicked innkeepers and brewers – had retreated to the half empty churches. When Lloyd George started on his extraordinary career, he was borne forward on a flood-tide of anti-alcohol oratory. 'Wine is a mocker. Strong drink is raging' – and the youthful Lloyd George easily outraged the drink. Teetotalism led to respectability, and respectability led to business success. The chain was complete.

Alas, even in the hey-day of Noncomformity, the Demon Drink still had his secret supporters in Wales. The pubs were officially closed on Sunday, but the local boozers always knew on which door to tap discreetly on a Sunday morning. As one publican explained to me, 'On Sunday we shut but we don't close, if you understand what I mean.' Indeed I did, for in the industrial areas – the mining valleys, the steel towns and the tin plate villages – an ingenious Sunday escape-hatch had flourished since the 1900s. Visitors to long-standing Labour strongholds in the valleys are sometimes astonished to find that the most florid building in the place bears the sign 'Conservative Club'. In theory, these are the product of the fund raised by the Tories to commemorate the great Lord Salisbury and to encourage the formation of Conservative centres throughout the country. In practice they are monuments to the ingenuity and determination of the average Welsh drinker. Nowhere was the memory of Lord Salisbury more fervently celebrated than in the mining valleys of South Wales, and the reason was simple. The Welfare Halls were high-minded organisations and would never apply for a Sunday club drinking licence. The Con Clubs had so such inhibitions. They applied for licences with gusto throughout industrial South Wales and many a successful Labour election campaign was planned over glasses of ale under the bearded photograph of the great Conservative statesman. Con Clubs indeed!

Still, the chapel teetotallers continued their eloquent campaign to draw their Nonconformist brethren's attention to the

sovereign powers of pure water or tea. Young men who left the chapels for the great adventure of becoming a draper in London or a milkman in Liverpool were always presented with the Little Red Book, containing not the thoughts of Chairman Mao but the anxious warnings of John Angell Jones against 'The Drink'. I still possess a copy of *Y Gwr Ieuanc Oddicatref – The Young Man Away from Home*, with its chapter headings outlining the 'fountains of peril' that lay in wait for the innocent adventurer into the dangers of England. John Angell warns him against the sin of entering a cigar divan in the Haymarket, of dancing at Cremorne Gardens and of riding in a hansom cab with a 'painted lady' down the Strand.

The work was first written in the 1860s but it continued to be published until the beginning of the First World War. My own copy is inscribed 'Presented to Tommy Jenkins by the church of Pen-y-Graig, February 1904'. I wondered what happened to Tommy, for although the well-intentioned John Angell Jones may have thought that he was warning his young readers against temptation, what he had actually produced was a complete guide to all the haunts of sin. Did Tommy Jenkins tuck his *Gwr Ieuanc Oddicatref* under his arm and head straight for the Haymarket? I bet he did. How the wicked persist in flourishing in spite of the cares of the godly! There were even back-sliders among the chapel teetotallers themselves. I remember a little ritual which was always performed when a certain minister of the Gospel, who was also a distinguished Welsh poet, called at our house. If he arrived with his wife, a keen supporter of the Woman's Temperance League, Mother would tactfully suggest, in the euphuistic phraseology of the time, that he might like to 'wash his hands'. My duty was to guide him to 'the place' but the route always led through Father's study where a bottle of Welsh whisky and a jug of water were conveniently placed. The dialogue was standardised. I would say, 'It is very cold. Would you take something for it?' The

71

minister would reply, 'Purely medicinal. Don't normally touch it – but since you press me.' He needed no pressing. A large tot of whisky disappeared down the poetic throat followed by a strong peppermint. As they would say in Wales, 'Ah well, just an unfortunate lapse.'

But that little memory from the distant past reveals one small thing about our household. In the midst of the Welsh teetotal desert it was a little oasis of quiet drinking. Everything in moderation, of course, for although Father did occasionally take a little whisky and kept some port in the cellar, they were used mainly for hospitality for visitors. It was not until I had reached seventeen that he first offered me a glass of whisky, heavily diluted with water, to mark my steady approach to man's estate, and strange to relate, the first drop of alcholic liquor that passed my lips was actually produced in Wales. Believe it or not, there was actually a time when Wales produced its own genuine malt whisky and it was sold by the wine merchants in my own home town of Swansea. Come to think of it, there was no reason at all why Wales should not have had its own distillery. Whisky is a Celtic drink and Wales possesses all the right ingredients for making it – barley grown on hill pastures, clear water flowing from peat deposits, and any amount of poets to sing the praises of the product. It only wanted a man of enterprise to arrive and strike whisky from the Welsh rock.

Squire Lloyd-Price of Rhiwlas, near Bala, was a great Welsh eccentric in the tradition that so delighted Thomas Love Peacock. A. J. Lloyd-Price Esq. would have been the ideal host for Headlong Hall. He was a sportsman who produced such memorable volumes as *Dogs Ancient and Modern*, *Walks in Wales* and *Rabbits for Powder and Rabbits for Profit*. He was a strong supporter of cottage industries and a keen student of pedigrees, both of men and of horses. In fact, at one stage in his career, he plunged heavily on the Cambridgeshire to recoup his fortunes. Rumour has it that this was the only occasion when prayers were offered up in lonely Welsh chapels for the success of a racehorse. Bendigo, with the fate of the Squire and most of Bala on his back, romped home in the race and the Squire never forgot his lucky escape.

Over the family vault in Llanfor churchyard he engraved this pious verse:

> As to my later end I go
> To meet my Jubilee,
> I bless the good horse Bendigo
> Who built this tomb for me.

It may have been Bendigo's money that helped to float the great dream of Welsh whisky. Squire Lloyd-Price and his associates were determined to do the thing properly. They built a solid, stone-walled distillery at Frongoch beside the river Treweryn. They bought the best machinery and hired experts from Speyside to supervise the work.

At last the great day dawned. Welsh whisky, decorated with a vivid label showing a lady in national costume sampling the contents with obvious relish, was placed on the market. History does not record that the Scottish distillers were unduly worried. They had faced such competition before. Scotch – genuine Scotch – has survived all attempts to imitate its peculiar qualities.

Alas, Welsh whisky proved no exception to the rule. I do not suggest that it was as curious as the product known as 'Himalayan Dew' which I once drank in India, or 'King George Black and White as Served by Queen Mary in Buckingham Palace', a Javanese whisky, but it did, according to one connoisseur who tasted it, possess a remarkable and unusual property – it matured backwards. It was splendid in the cask, and puzzling, to say the least of it, in the bottle.

The squire did his best to push it on the market. He prepared a special cask which he sent to King Edward VII when he was Prince of Wales. The royal secretary, in a courteous acknowledgement, intimated that the Prince was pleased to keep Welsh whisky in his cellar. There is no record of its ever coming out!

I have a picture in my mind of the gallant squire arriving at the local inn and demanding whisky. A drop of Scotch is placed before him. 'Degenerate son of Wales!' he apostrophises the shame-faced landlord. 'How dare you serve me with this foreign concoction. I demand Welsh whisky. And if you haven't got it, sign here on this order book and I'll see that you'll get it – tomorrow!'

Perhaps it was his determination to popularise Welsh whisky that led the squire to promote a special table water which could go with it. I have an advertisement for it before me, ingeniously printed in the form of a railway ticket:

RHIWLAS ST BEUNO
SPARKLING DIURETIC TABLE WATER
THE NICEST OF ALL; AND THE KIDNEY AND LIVER PACIFICATOR
MIXES BEAUTIFULLY WITH WHITE WINE, LEMON OR SPIRITS.
2/6 PER DOZEN. CARRIAGE PAID BOTH WAYS.

I am a little worried about that persuasive phrase 'Liver and Kidney Pacificator'. Could the squire have designed Rhiwlas St Beuno to be taken *after* and not *before* Welsh whisky? But the First World War put an end to the squire's dream. His distillery at Frongoch became a prisoner-of-war camp for the prisoners of the Irish Easter Rising in 1916, including Michael Collins. He left no record of his opinion of Welsh whisky.

The Frongoch distillery itself was demolished and a few miles upstream from the site, the bull-dozers have created a new dam which impounds the waters of the Treweryn stream in order to supply Liverpool with water. At long last water was united with Welsh whisky.

There are still a few bottles left of Welsh whisky, guarded with care as a memorial to a glorious episode in the Welsh past, but I doubt if any bottles survive of the first great attempt to produce Welsh wine. No Frenchman would ever believe it, but there was a time, within my own memory, when the vines grew in ordered rows on a Glamorgan hillside, and the great carts, loaded with grapes, creaked their way in September along the banks of the river Taff and the new wine frothed and fermented in vast vats in the very heart of Cardiff. I must admit that the man who worked this miracle was not a Welshman but a Scot. A Celt all the same, and a romantic one at that.

James Patrick Crichton-Stuart, Third Marquess of Bute, was without question one of the most gifted of our Victorian noblemen, an authority on Coptic church symbolism and Scottish heraldry, a convert to the Roman Catholic church, a leading investigator of psychical phenomena and the translator of Turgenev. But his greatest gift was undoubtedly the millions left to him by his father, who had made a fortune out of Welsh coal. This was in the great days of the South Wales coalfield when the Rhondda was a black Klondike as the rival coal-owners fought like robber barons over mining options and railway lines to the sea. The Marquess – or rather his estate – was in the thick of the fight but clearly his heart was not in it. He was an eccentric and a dreamer and valued the coal-trucks filled with 'Best Welsh' that rattled down from the valleys only because they allowed him to give reality to his dreams.

Like all rich Victorian romantics he was passionate about building – in the Gothic style, naturally; he demanded towers, battlements, crenellations and all the architectural bric-à-brac of the Middle Ages – anything to shut out the view of Victorian

Cardiff. He got them in full measure from his architect, William Burges. Together they converted Cardiff Castle into a Roman fort with a Welsh Carcassonne stuck on the western wall. They then looked round for further ruins to conquer. They found what they were looking for at Taff's Well, some five miles north of Cardiff. Here the river Taff breaks through a line of high, limestone hills in a narrow gorge. The coalfield and its industry are out of sight and the hills are densely wooded.

Perched on a crag near the gorge were the ruins of Castell Coch, the Red Castle, built by one of the Welsh princes or an invading Norman baron to dominate the Glamorgan plain.

There are few written records of the castle's history and that made Burges's task all the more delightful. He and his patron could give full reign to their antiquarian enthusiasm. In 1871 they cleared the site and at last there arose a romantic turreted reconstruction that looked, for all the world, like the castles pictured on old hock labels. There was a drawbridge that worked – so well, in fact, that it once shot half a Sunday School treat into the dry moat.

As the marquess gazed with pride on his new castle, he could not fail to recognise how closely the site resembled the slopes of the Rhine, the Moselle or the Loire. Clearly there was only one thing wanting to make the picture perfect – a vineyard at the castle gate. When you have the Bute millions behind you it is possible to order a vineyard as the rest of us order a new car; the marquess had made his decision and the biggest vineyard ever planted in Britain in modern times started to grow on a steep hillside in Wales.

I am not sure if the marquess was a wine connoisseur. I suspect that he looked at the site, realised that it demanded a vineyard, and like a true artist determined to place one there. He searched the pages of the Venerable Bede, William of Malesbury and Geraldus Cambrensis for details of wine-growing in Britain in the Middle Ages. His vineyard, like his castle, was to be a grand gesture of defiance against the increasing materialism of his age. But he did not rely on the Venerable Bede for technical advice. Like Squire Lloyd-Price with his whisky, the marquess invited experts from the Continent to start the experiment. In 1875 he had the slopes below Castell Coch planted with vines in rows three feet apart. The experts declared that the soil had a superficial resemblance to the soils of the Haut Médoc, but actually it was a light fibrous loam overlying limestone. There was a long period of trial and error before it was finally decided to plant only one variety of vine, the Gamay Noir. The grapes were cultivated on the low stem system as used in most of the French vineyards. The marquess had every right to hope that he would soon be drinking his own wine, seated in his medieval armchair before a roaring fire in the guard room of Castell Coch, with the drawbridge up and a noble tome of Coptic liturgy to lend savour to the evening.

But in the world of wine you can never rely on your bottle until you have actually drunk it. Although he spent money lavishly and planned on a scale that would have made your modern British wine-growing enthusiast green with envy, he reckoned without Welsh weather. The Castell Coch site looked perfect for the job on a sunny day in early summer. You might easily imagine the grapes ripening happily and the Welsh *vignerons* singing – in four-part harmony, of course – as they tended the vines before going to choir practice in the nearby chapel. But, unfortunately, such days are rare. As one old Welsh countryman reminded me, 'Never forget that Welsh weather is teetotal.'

Mr Pettigrew, who was in charge of the experiment, ruefully admitted long afterwards that, 'The really experimental time for the vineyards of Castle Coch had been the worst we could have hit on for the last twenty or thirty years.' The marquess was unshaken. He acted on the principle that if you operate on a large enough scale you were bound to succeed. He simply ordered, 'Plant more vineyards.' At last he did achieve some success. In 1897 the wines were actually placed on the market through the well-known firm of Messrs Hatch, Mansfield and Co. The catalogue listed them as 'Welsh Wines: Canary Brand', and was somewhat coy about their quality, simply stating that, 'Although these wines cannot be said to possess the delicate aroma and flavour of the best foreign wines, they are eminently wholesome and honest.' Not a very glowing encomium!

But this was a marked improvement on *Punch*'s comment that it would take four men to drink a bottle of this wine, two to hold the victim down, and one to pour it down his throat!

I came on the scene far too late to sample Château Cardiff but I remember that my uncle once had a bin of the 1892 in his cellar and he gave me his opinion. 'It is some time since I sampled them, my boy. The marquess was a great authority on Coptic literature and a fine gentleman. Let us leave it at that.' But it is only fair to say that other judges went on record with a more favourable opinion, declaring that the Bute vintages were 'luscious, golden wines, resembling first-class champagne', and again 'with an aroma far in advance of grape wines manufactured in the country'. Manufactured? A curious word, indeed.

All I can add to these pronouncements from the past is that the labels on the bottles were splendid, no matter what the contents tasted like. I remember admiring them in my uncle's cellar, where he kept them as historic curiosities – they had a William Morris-Walter Crane air about them, all turrets and tangled vine-leaves. Both red and white wines were made but no distinctive names were given to wines of different natures. The labels maintained a tactful silence about the contents of the bottles and simple indicated that they came from the Bute vineyards.

The wine promise of the nineties, like so much else of the period, did not last. Welsh wine was definitely a *fin de siècle* curiosity. Soon the weather was 'at it again'; the Third Marquess died and his son carried on, but the vintages remained uncertain. By 1914 the Butes had to confess defeat. By 1920 the vines had disappeared from the slopes below the Red Castle and now only grass covers the greatest Welsh vineyard. In the dark vaults of Cardiff Castle the vats gathered dust and the remaining bottles were left undisturbed through the Second World War. Then an expert from Messrs Harveys of Bristol was

79

called in to pronounce on the last of the Bute wine. He raised a glass to his lips and pronounced the fatal word, 'Vinegar'.

The great dream of a Welsh Côte d'Or was over.

I lament the fact that, although Welsh whisky passed my lips when I was young, Welsh wine never did. For, in truth, I never entered the world of wine until I went up to Oxford, ostensibly with a scholarship to read history, but looking back on it, the generous university was also prepared to give me tuition in a whole range of the arts of civilised living, including sex and, above all, wine. For the Oxford I timorously entered on that memorable Michaelmas term in 1927 was as remote as the moon from modern Oxford, with its trendy dons refusing honorary degrees to Prime Ministers, its co-educational colleges, its jeans-clad undergraduates training for the next protest march.

My Oxford was still a survivor from the privileged past which had not yet been dragged, protesting, into the grim, bleak future. The consequences of the First World War had not yet worked through to the collegiate establishment. Members of Magadalen wine clubs could still jump out of their windows into the Cherwell and swim about in full evening dress with no one regarding it as singular. Undergraduates still wore gowns and mortar boards if they went out after 9 p.m. and they had to be back in college before the deep bell of Great Tom in the tower of Christchurch struck midnight. The Proctors and their 'bulldogs' still patrolled the town after dark and fined undergraduates who drank in the local pubs. Ladies were only allowed in men's colleges in the afternoons, and we still had to pass examinations in Latin and Divinity before we could continue our studies. On the surface, it was still the Oxford to which my father had won his scholarship in 1895.

Even the Oxford jokes he told me were still valid, including the classic story of the dashing undergraduate who was stopped by the Proctors as he was escorting a certain 'lady of

the town'. The Proctors went through the prescribed ritual,
'Will you please introduce us to this lady?' 'Certainly,' came
the reply, 'Messrs Proctors – my sister.' The Proctors were
astonished. 'Are you aware, sir, that your "sister" is the most
notorious prostitute in Oxford?' 'Yes,' said the dashing undergraduate, 'Mother and I are quite worried about it.'

We still attended compulsory early morning chapel on a
certain number of mornings a week, and I found myself in my
first week gazing at the very same lectern, with its great bronze
eagle supporting the Bible, which had featured in one of my
father's favourite stories. A certain friend of his, who as a
scholar had to read one of the morning lessons, had spent a
somewhat alcoholic time of it the night before. His friends
managed to get him up and into the chapel but he was still in a

somewhat muzzy state. When the moment of truth came he managed to get to the lectern and hang on to it for support but the words danced before his eyes. 'And Jesus said . . .' he began bravely, and then the text went out of focus. He began again, 'And Jesus said . . .' but again the text disappeared. Then his cry of despair echoed through the chapel. 'If this bloody bird would stop waggling his tail, I'd tell you what Jesus said.' He disappeared for the rest of the term – or, in the Oxford term of the day, he was 'rusticated'.

How remote it all sounds today! Yet, as Talleyrand said about the *ancien régime*, those who never lived through it have never known the *douceur de vivre*. I put a little toe into that privileged pool. Selfishly I don't regret it.

Some of the dons of my day were worthy of the name. They were soon to be pushed off the stage by the smarter, more leftish dons of the 1930s, but when I arrived there were still survivors from before the First World War – Bellocian dons, 'Regal Dons' –

> Compact of ancient tales and port
> And sleep – and learning of a sort.

Classical learning, of course, for a First in classics was still the blue ribband of Oxford education, your sure passport to a brilliant career in the higher Civil Service. I had obviously dodged the column by proposing to read history. This was clear from my first interview with that curious figure, my moral tutor. My history tutor would be my chief contact with the teaching staff but the college also provided a second don who, presumably, would look after my morals, such as they were, throughout my Oxford career. There was probably a clause in the founder's charter, given in the fourteenth century, which provided for a *magister* who would see that those *in statu pupilari* attended mass and behaved in a 'lawful and decent manner on saints' days'. Over the centuries, the moral tutorship dwindled to a formality – a pleasant welcome to the newly arrived and nervous youngest member of the college.

My moral tutor was a classical scholar, a true Bellocian don of impressive amplitude, who received me with a decanter of vintage port and two glasses on the table before him. 'Now, let me see. You are going to read history.' (He pronounced the word with some distaste.) 'I think you would have done better to read classics.' He poured me out a glass of port. 'After all, what is history? Just divine gossip about the past among gentlemen. Taste your port.' He poured a glass for himself, and carefully sniffed it and slowly rolled it over his tongue.

'Dow's 1896, and still excellent. What do you think?' Oh, the flattery of it! Here was I, who had never tasted a vintage port before in my life, being asked to pronounce on what I now know was one of the great ports of all time.

At nineteen, my palate was frankly non-existent. It had not even started on its long development into the litmus-paper tongue of the true connoisseur. Many years of conscientious and cultured drinking would be required before I could pronounce with confidence on such a port. Yet, clearly, some words were expected from me; and it was then, by utter luck, that I stumbled upon the vital trick that all who pretend to wine expertise must learn when confronted with a great vintage.

For example, your host has poured out with pride a glass of wine of obvious importance on which he expects, not only your general opinion, but an accurate analysis of the year and the château. After all, you have now built up some slight pretensions as a 'man of wine'. Your reputation is at stake as you spin the wine in the glass – *dodeliner*, or 'nursing', is the expressive French word for this essential opening move. Then you assess the perfume or 'nose' released by this swinging movement and finally carefully roll the first mouthful over the tongue.

The golden rule is never to make a judgement straight away. Play for time. Pause. Spin the wine again and re-test the 'nose'. Then look up at your host, smile gently and utter a resounding, flattering but totally non-committal comment. 'Fascinating,' you might say, 'fascinating . . . absolutely fascinating.' Or perhaps, 'Remarkable, remarkable!' With a bit of luck you may find that your host, ·flattered by your enthusiasm, may even drop an unconscious hint, on which you seize with avidity. Now you feel your way forward. 'Could it be a St Julien, no, no, maybe a Paulliac?' If your host betrays a smile you can now proceed with confidence. It would most certainly

84

not be a Latour, Lafite or Mouton-Rothschild – your host is not a millionaire – so the bet is that it is a *deuxième cru*. You know that there are only two *deuxième crus* in Paulliac, so take a plunge on one. 'Pichon-Longueville.' Then running through the good years you risk 1971. Your host is delighted and your reputation is safe. A final golden rule. Never overplay your luck. Rest on your laurels. Let someone else appraise the next bottle!

But all this lay in the future on that early autumn evening in 1927 when my moral tutor awaited my comments on the 1890 port. I hunted desperately for an adjective and then blurted out, 'It's noble.' He smiled, 'Indeed it is. You'll remember this noble wine when you, too, are as old as this port.' Then he added, 'Pity. You should have read classics. We do have a better choice of wine.'

As I walked back to my rooms through the darkening quad I felt I had passed a milestone in my life. There was a pleasant glow in my stomach – no, I hadn't got tight on my first glass as the teetotal propagandists suggested, but the world did seem a better place. I hadn't started on the slippery path to eternal damnation. Rather had I found a new, secret pleasure in life. Of course, I didn't drink port of that quality throughout my college career. In fact, I only drank another glass of it at the dinner our tutor gave us after we had sat our final examinations. That sort of port was the privilege of the dons, and certain colleges – not necessarily the biggest or more aristocratic among them – acquired a certain prestige and fame for the quality of the port they had laid down. Pembroke is a small college, lost in the shadow of Christchurch, and Dr Johnson its only illustrious son. But 'Pemmy Port' had a great reputation, and many a keen port-lover intrigued for an invitation to dine at Pembroke High Table, to be followed by a session over the port in the Senior Common Room.

Was it the same when Dr Johnson was an undergraduate? Long afterwards, he pontificated that wine was the drink for boys but port was the drink for men. He also added that brandy was the drink for heroes, but I think he added that bit about brandy to give a final flourish to the sentence. Port for men! Did the youthful Johnson also have a moral tutor who initiated him into the glories of 'Pemmy Port'? If so, he – like me – would only have got a few memorable glasses of it, for he was even poorer than I was when he came up to Oxford.

It was cash, after all, that limited my exploration of this new, exciting world of wine. Like Keats I could only try what was within my price range. We drank the cheaper college wines, breezily labelled Pommard or St Emilion, for the Beaujolais business hadn't started in my early days. I am sure, however, that those magisterial dons who had laid down their own port with such care, saw to it that our wines were at least wholesome and good value for money. And as I drank them, I became aware that there were greater glories awaiting me as soon as I got the cash. I was still an innocent but I had made a start.

I can see myself now, with a small group of similarly innocent friends, coming out after dinner in Hall and daringly ordering a crème de menthe from the buttery. On warm summer evenings we would sit on the Hall steps and feel that we were really living the sophisticated life as we sipped our somewhat sticky liqueur and smoked – of all things – Balkan Sobranie cigarettes. For Oxford had

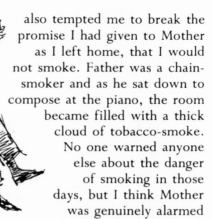

also tempted me to break the promise I had given to Mother as I left home, that I would not smoke. Father was a chain-smoker and as he sat down to compose at the piano, the room became filled with a thick cloud of tobacco-smoke. No one warned anyone else about the danger of smoking in those days, but I think Mother was genuinely alarmed at the scale of Father's cigarette consumption. She need not have worried about me, for I never became a true smoker. I never succeeded in inhaling and kept tapping the ash off my cigarette as it smouldered in my hand, with disastrous results. Sooner or later the tip flew off and lodged among the sofa's cushions. Hostesses began to look at me askance. The climax of my smoking saga came during the war, not so many months before I had found myself landing in the south of France.

I had gone with a colleague, Stewart Macpherson, to report on our submarine war. We had a rough time at sea and came back to base at Blyth to celebrate rather too well in the ward room. Macpherson was to return to London and I was due to catch a midnight train at Newcastle and travel overnight to join our agricultural expert, Roy Hay, on the island of Arran in the Firth of Clyde so that we could report on the war effort of the Arran farmers to increase their output. From submarines to potatoes – commentating in wartime Britain certainly didn't lack contrasts! Due to the celebrations in the ward room, our generous host had forgotten to lay on the duty car. No matter. They put a cordon across the road and stopped the night bus that ran through the blacked-out countryside to Newcastle station. To ease the tension, I lit a cigarette as we sat in the

darkened bus and eventually the inevitable happened. I tapped the cigarette and away went the burning tip. Opposite us was an RAF sergeant and his girl, too busy in the blackout to notice that there were any other passengers. To my horror the tip described a fiery curve and lodged itself at the top of the sergeant's trousers in the one spot where I could not have removed it without my intentions being seriously misunderstood. Horrified, I saw a wisp of rising smoke, indicating a dangerous threat to the sergeant's most intimate personal possessions.

I looked around for help. The conductress was almost on her knees laughing. I looked outside and a blue light appeared in the darkness. A police station. I leapt up, rang the bell and, followed by Macpherson, scrambled off the bus. It disappeared into the darkness carrying the sergeant and my still burning cigarette tip. I can only hope he discovered it in time before it qualified him for the most extraordinary war wound in the Second World War. The police and the BBC were allies in those days. A patrol car drove us to Newcastle station; the strange crowded wartime station full of troops waiting for the next train, canteens dispensing powerfully sweet tea, a chaos being desperately sorted out by harassed Transport Officers. At last I found my train and wedged myself into the crowded compartment next to the window. 'Have a cigarette?' wickedly suggested Macpherson, who was seeing me off. 'No, no,' I said, 'I think I ought to give up.' 'Go on,' insisted Macpherson and weakly I lit up.

What followed was almost standard procedure by now. The train began to move, I flicked my cigarette and away went the tip to land, this time, in the folds of a newspaper someone was trying to read in the hooded light. The wind from the moving train fanned the tip and the newspaper burst into flames. It seemed that everyone in that crowded compartment was equipped with something combustible. If it wasn't a newspaper it was wrappings for fish and chips. In a moment I was engulfed in a mass of furious men beating out flames and calling down every form of curse on my hapless head.

Macpherson had seen what was happening from the platform and could hardly wait until he got back to London and burst in on the office of Michael Standing, who was then head of Outside Broadcasts. Together they sent off a witty telegram to Roy Hay who was waiting for me in Arran, 'Beware arrival of Von Thomas, suspected incendiarist'. Wit is always dangerous in wartime. Within half an hour the telegram had been intercepted by Security and lay on the desk of the Director General of the BBC, while an embarrassed Standing tried to explain that it was all a joke.

When I, in turn, stepped off the boat on Lamlash Pier I found a white-faced Roy Hay standing between two stern, shoulder-padded, and very tough-looking Navy security men. 'Von Thomas?' they said. 'Yes.' 'Come with us', and they escorted me into the little hut at the end of the pier. 'You are aware that this island is a major storage point for vital naval ammunition. What is the meaning of this?' And they produced a copy of Michael Standing's unlucky telegram. I stammered in astonishment. 'Well, I know nothing about this. All I did was light a cigarette!'

Of course, my explanations finally dissolved in laughter and drinks all round at the nearest hotel, but it definitely finished my inglorious career as a cigarette smoker. I had no need for government warnings. To have run the danger of blowing up the whole of the naval ammunition on the island of Arran was enough.

But in those early days at Oxford, the aroma of Balkan Sobranie, full of eastern promise, seemed to admit me to a new world of exotic experience, seasoned with a sense of deliciously forbidden sin. Mother, and even John Angell Jones, were not alone in their warnings about the danger of cigarettes. We had a pious neighbour in Swansea delivering tracts to all the houses within range. Every Easter a new 'Message of Love to the Sons and Daughters of Wales' shot into our letter-box dealing with some particularly insidious and tempting sin. I'm afraid the message fell on stony ground for the tracts were valued, not for their content, but for the extraordinary staccato style in which they were written, ending with a verse that, the good lady felt, was bound to drive home the message. It so happened that the Message of Love for the year in which I went up to Oxford dealt with 'The Smoking' and ended with the memorable verse:

> Fie, ministers in filth so deep!
> Angels look down and then they weep;
> Jesus they preach to other folk,
> And children ask 'Did Jesus smoke?'

Unanswerable! A cloud of Balkan Sobranie smoke slowly eclipses the scene.

My Oxford career ended in what I felt at the time to be a personal disaster but now, looking back on it, it was simply a completion of my education. I got my degree with a certain

91

amount of panache and the world, I concluded, lay wide open before me. I decided on the higher Civil Service – especially India. As I prepared for the examination, I saw a glorious career ahead; a district to administer somewhere in the Punjab

perhaps, with endless opportunities for climbing in the Himalayas. I had become a mountaineering fanatic at university and dreamt of amazing adventures among the Mother of the Snows. Today the Himalayas are overrun by expeditions. They queue up for permits and didn't a Japanese actually try to ski down Everest? Fifty years ago the great peaks, from K2 to Kanchenjunga, were untrodden. Hundreds of lesser summits were untouched, waiting for me to immortalise my name with a first ascent. Yes, I had it all planned as I sat in the examination room at Burlington House.

In those days the test was divided into two parts, the written examination and the interview. Equal importance was attached to both sections. I did brilliantly in the written section but the interview was another matter. The moghuls of the Establishment looked at me and unanimously decided, 'This man will never govern Bengal.' Of course they were right. Myself as a Kiplingesque administrator? I can chuckle, now, at the very idea, but at the time I was devastated. I had no option but to retreat to South Wales. Farewell the vintage port, a long farewell to my early explorations of claret, hock and burgundy. I had to *reculer pour mieux sauter* – I fell back to the outer fringe of the serious drinking world. I embarked on my beer period!

Beer! What a contrast to the Château-Grillet that I was savouring on the terrace at Les Baux with my knowledgeable French officer – the scene that had inspired me to embark on my vinous memoirs. All aspiring young wine students, I am convinced, pass through their beer period, however much they might wish to conceal it. But Les Baux was clearly not the place to discuss my adventures with beer. In any case, the critical point of the campaign was approaching. The French had been pushing the Germans out of the plain of Provence into the narrow jaws of the Rhône valley. Now was the time for the Americans to swoop down from the Route Napoleon that they had been following in the mountains and fling themselves across the line of the German retreat in the valley. The enemy would be neatly placed in the bag.

The chosen point of interception lay just north of the town of Montélimar. The Americans had studied every military eventuality. They knew the German strength precisely, the rate at which their columns moved, their total lack of air support and the exact amount of ammunition they had left. There was only one gap in their appreciation of the situation. They had forgotten the gastronomic factor.

Admirably as the American intelligence officers had acquitted themselves, they did not contain keen food and wine lovers among their numbers. French intelligence, on the other hand, was securely based on the hard gastronomic facts of life. They were well aware of a hidden peril that lay ahead. The town of

Montélimar is famous as the capital of nougat. In the middle of the sixteenth century, Olivier de Serres had successfully introduced almond plants from the Middle East and had established almond orchards north of Montélimar. To the south lay the plentiful honey of Provence. At the very same time that Nostradamus was producing his treatise on perfumes and meditating on his *Centuries* the ingenious citizens of Montélimar were busy on the delicate business of marrying the almond paste to the honey. They produced nougat, and by the end of the nineteenth century Montélimar was the nougat capital of the world.

The factories and warehouses were full of this delicious sweetmeat as the first American tanks rolled in. They were all set to cut directly across the line of the German retreat; but at this decisive moment the gastronomic factor took over and disaster struck. The American bombardment had set a nougat factory on fire on the outskirts of the town. A sticky flood of the sweetmeat now poured across the road. It was the Germans' secret weapon and no anti-tank mine could approach its deadly effectiveness. In a matter of seconds the sticky nougat had entangled the tank tracks and the mighty Sherman tanks – the pride of the American armoured divisions – ground to a halt. The commander of the leading tank jumped out and then shouted in incredulity, 'The bastards have tied us up with chewing gum!' The shade of Olivier de Serres must have shuddered off stage. Nougat compared to chewing gum! After that, the Germans almost deserved to escape. They didn't get off scot-free, however. They had to abandon their horse transport, cars and even a steam train they were trying to run on the railway. By the time I came to it, the road north of Montélimar was a hideous shambles of dead horses, burnt-out cars and abandoned munition lorries. But the infantry had got away – no doubt with every man clutching a box of looted nougat as a symbol of his escape.

How the fate of nations turn on trivia! Professional historians frown disapprovingly on what they call the Cleopatra's

nose theory of history, the suggestion that the whole course of
Roman history, for example, was changed by Antony's infatu-
ation with the Serpent of the Old Nile – but what would have
happened if Cleopatra had been a long-nosed frump? Or take
an example nearer home. It is generally agreed that the House
of Tudor was one of the greatest dynasties to occupy the
English throne, culminating in the glories of the Elizabethan
age. But would the Tudors have ever been heard of if Katherine
of France, the widow of Henry V, had not looked out of the

window of her apartment at Windsor Castle, and saw an obscure but handsome young Welsh squire bathing in the nude with some of his friends in the Thames below? As one chronicler reported: 'She was struck by the beauty and power of his person.' I bet she was! They were secretly married and their eldest son, Edmund, became the father of Henry Tudor, the future Henry VII. Surely never has sexual attraction played such a decisive part in English history. Supposing young Owen Tudor had been an averagely gifted man instead of the champion Welsh sexual athlete, would we have had the glories of the Elizabethan age? Who can tell?

After Montélimar I retired frustrated to French HQ to file my despatch. As I came out I met a familiar figure. It was the Colonel. 'How glad I am to see you,' he boomed. 'Between you and me, old chap, they've rumbled me. I've been recalled. Ah, well, it couldn't have lasted. But I've decided to have one good swan before I go. Come with me.' My news opportunities had gone for the moment. Lyons would be the next big story, but before that there were the Rhône vineyards. The Colonel was incredulous. 'Vineyards! Wine! That's no story. The British don't want wine. Tell you what – give 'em horses. That's the stuff. Horses. They'll lap them up.'

Maybe he had something. In the wake of the Montélimar disappointment, I found myself ferrying across the wide Rhône at Arles, turning my back for the moment on the war and driving out over the vast, horse-haunted level, the lake-scattered plain of that most fascinating part of Provence – the Carmargue.

CHAPTER FOUR

Sidetracked
by Beer

The Camargue is really the western section of the delta of the river Rhône. The great river is now guided out to its final rest in the sea through a series of high-banked channels, but not before it has spread out a vast alluvial plain dotted with shallow lakes. A hidden, surprising part of France which remained lost and almost unknown to the rest of the country until the middle of the nineteenth century.

We drove into the heart of it over roads that had become grass-grown during the German occupation. The Germans had cleared everybody back from the actual coast but had left the manadiers, the owners of the great farms of the Camargue, undisturbed. The German army was highly mechanised at its fighting tip but it still needed a surprising amount of horses for its supply columns. These great farmers of the Camargue had long been famous as horse breeders. Their troops of white horses wandered at will over the marshlands and through the shallow water of the lagoons. Great roseate flights of flamingos moved lazily over the marshes; the glittering silver channels of the waterways were fringed with a feathered embroidery of waving reeds and, away in the distance, the blue line of the Alpine foothills. Beyond them, somewhere over the horizon, the war was still going on. For a few blissful days, we had opted out.

Here in the heart of the Camargue we were lapped in a deep consoling silence. For a moment the war had turned time backwards. All the modern excrescences that our restless age had dragged into the Camargue had been temporarily eliminated. We were seeing the country as it was a hundred·years ago and the sight was consoling indeed. The Colonel was delighted. 'This is the life – almost like India. And those horses! Don't think they'd do on the huntin' field, but what fire – what spirit!' And we watched a troop go past us at speed, dashing through the shallows, the spray rising in flashing fountains from their hooves, and the mares and foals lifting their heads in a wild, tossing rhythm to get out of the spray. I got carried away. 'This is poetry,' I shouted to the Colonel, 'Poetry you can see!'

It wasn't until I was fifty, and long after the war, that I

actually rode on a horse, but it was the sight of those white horses thundering through the bright shallows of the Camargue that inspired me to take to the saddle myself at an absurdly advanced age. I have never regretted it.

I do regret, however, that I ever went back to the Camargue after the war. I wish I had always remembered it as the land where time had turned back. But the BBC proposed a programme on the Camargue and I was tempted. Would it really have changed? It had, with a vengeance. This was 1965 and tourism was in full swing. The lagoons, the horses, the flamingos were still there but, somehow, the spirit had gone. We were the guests of one of the most famous of the *manadiers*, Denys Colomb. We drove along the verge of the largest lagoon where the flamingos were standing on one leg in the shallows. Denys had just taken part in the film *'Crin' Blanc'* ('White Mane') that had featured his most famous stallion, and the middle-aged lady reporter from Rouen who was with us asked the question that no French journalist can resist. What about sex? 'All your stallions run with the herd. How can you tell which one creates the offspring?'

'But easily,' said Denys. 'There can only be one stallion – the strongest, who fights like a fiend for his love rights. My "Crin' Blanc" is magnificent. The other day he scented the

nostrils of a pair of young stallions wrinkle at a quarter of a mile distance; he tore after them in a flash. The fights between stallions are terrific, but you cannot appreciate the splendour of a stallion until you see him at the moment of love. Then his eyes flash fire, every line of his muscles stands out, he is the furious embodiment of the Life Force. I am filming this and matching it, as in a ballet, to noble music.'

The French lady reporter sighed, 'How well I understand the inspiration behind that work of art.'

But there was no doubt that the post-war Camargue had started to change. Will the last paradise of the horse disappear as the vast Mondragon power schemes on the Rhône drain the marshes and rice farms displace the flamingos?

'Will they leave us nothing, these damned engineers?' fulminated Denys Colomb, as his cowboys came riding up from the horses to escort our car, like a troop of lancers escorting the old Viceroy of India. 'Rice culture indeed! The man who plants rice is the most inelegant of peasants; his life is spent bottom-up grubbing in the mud. Contrast the row of advancing posteriors with the free carriage and upright glance of my horsemen of the Camargue. We are being engineered into insignificance. We do not want to become the slaves of co-operatives; we must reject these tempters. We must be the last place left in this France of the cheap car, the power line and the massed tourists where you can come and say, "Here I will still see man in his natural state, religious, drunk, talkative, believing in honour and fearing pain and death."'

I remember that, at the time, I was deeply impressed by those words. It is a Welsh weakness. We are a nation brought up to believe that eloquence is important. When a man doesn't speak easily we distrust him. 'Doesn't say much. Wonder what he is thinking behind our backs,' we murmur. I couldn't help thinking what the Colonel would have made of Denys's oratory if he could have heard it. A rich snort of incredulity, probably. For, alas, that picture of the future was an impossible dream. Mass tourism has returned. The great estates were bound to be turned into dude ranches. 50,000 francs a week and all found, including a bull fight and a descendant of Crin' Blanc in action. Said Denys's manager to me in a revealing aside, 'Down here we are already living a picture-postcard life.' And he introduced me to a splendid survivor from the old days known as Clan-Clan, a magnificent white-bearded ancient who had once been a waiter in the café painted by Van Gogh. 'You must have known and seen him often,' I said. 'Tell me what he was like.'

Clan-Clan sighed through his white beard. 'But there were so many artists, monsieur. We just fed them. And it wasn't like today; we did not think of tourism.'

Nor did the Colonel and I, on those few days when the war had for a short moment turned time back and restored the old Camargue. We drove down to the sea, for hadn't the pre-war guidebooks warned us, 'Those who do not visit Les Saintes-Maries-de-la-Mer cannot understand the soul of the Camargue.' I doubt if the Colonel was interested in the soul part but he liked the idea of going down to the sea. 'Maybe we'll find something to drink there other than wine,' he murmured. The little township lies close to the mouth of the Rhône, protected from the sea by a dike. The central attraction is the fortified church built to celebrate the supposed arrival, on this very spot in 40 AD of the Virgin Mary and her sister, Mary, the mother of St James the Lesser. You have to hand it to those ingenious churchmen of the early Middle Ages. When they needed a saint, they didn't hesitate to grab the most impressive one available in the calendar. And there were no spoil-sport reporters like myself around in 40

AD to ruin a good story. The church became a lucrative place of pilgrimage, and even added to its attractions by being host to the gypsies of France on a special festival day in honour of the gypsies' patron saint, Sara. Great tourist stuff.

All this disappeared during the German occupation and the gypsies were certainly wise to make themselves scarce. When we arrived, the inhabitants were starting to struggle back to their homes. The Café des Bohémiens was reopening. The indomitable proprietor, who had managed to get a horse and cart, was busy putting bottles on the shelves stripped bare by the departing Germans. The little township had been knocked about a bit in the closing stages of the occupation. He was delighted to see us. 'Life will now return to normal after madness.' He beamed as we sat down at the cast-iron table and

became the first tourists of 1944 – and, at that moment, the only ones in sight. The Colonel had looked along the shelves, now being re-stocked with all those mysterious liqueurs that only French stomachs can relish. 'No sign of a G-and-T, leave alone whisky,' he sighed, and had resigned himself to a glass of Provençal wine when the proprietor reappeared and placed two bottles on the table. 'Would you prefer this?' he asked. Beer! 'Unfortunately we have no refrigerator. It is not cold.' No matter. The Colonel was delighted. Here was a return to British drinking standards at last.

As the Colonel drinks his luke-warm beer and I sip my wine, here, surely, is the time for me to produce my next diversion – the next section of my vinous memoirs. We have slipped away for the moment from the world of wine. I can now confess to my Beer Period.

All young men drink beer at some time or other. I first drank it – like so many other firsts in my life – at Oxford. When I was engaged in violent exercise, my body seemed easily able to absorb a pint or two without noticing it. And beer seemed to go naturally with sport. Take mountaineering, for example. You don't call for a carefully decanted bottle of Pichon-Longueville '61 when you come back to your mountain inn after a day spent balancing on small holds on the great slab of Clogwyn Du'r Arddu in Snowdonia with a 400-foot drop below you. No, you clamour for a Newcastle Brown or a Worthington E.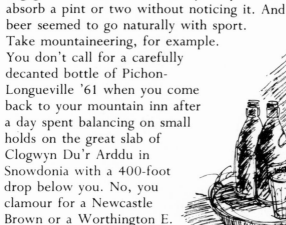

In the same way, beer seemed the only proper drink that

suited the first job I had when I retreated back to South Wales from Oxford. I became an area officer for the Council of Social Service. The mining valleys were in the cruel grip of that first great depression of the 1930s. I was charged with the task of giving grants to the clubs for the unemployed that had sprung up to give some sort of rallying places to the men and women living in the despair of the dole. It was my second education – Oxford in complete reverse – and I am profoundly grateful to the mining valleys for teaching me the realities of life, and, above all, the courage and comradeship of communities under travail.

I would meet the committee in the local and the drinks were always chalked up to me. It was then that I imbibed, along with the beer, the vital South Wales doctrine of the Unfortunate Lapse. Sooner or later the chairman would take me aside and say, 'Can I have a quiet word with you? We'd better slip into the back bar.'

Then came the inevitable confession. 'Mr Thomas, I'm sorry to tell you – there's been an unfortunate lapse. Dai Williams, our treasurer – just a little confusion between the red and black columns. Could have happened to any one of us. Last heard of in Porthcawl, poor dab. His wife's in a pitiful state.' Then the conspiratorial whisper. 'Mr Thomas, you're one of us now. We know that we can rely on you.'

Indeed they could. Impossible to blame the treasurer for yielding to temptation and grabbing a short glimpse of happiness, even if it was with government money. We closed ranks and I managed another grant. It was for the magnificent amount of £20. I hope that government auditors will never plough through those records of my financial transactions of the 1930s. How can I explain that the item earmarked for library books was actually the £1 2s. 6d. expended on beer for the boys? Perhaps I can put it down, for once, as a Fortunate Lapse.

My second fortunate lapse in my Beer Period was in complete contrast to my re-education in the mining valleys. I began my friendship with my fellow townsman, poet and dedicated beer-drinker, Dylan Thomas. I had first met Dylan at the Swansea Grammar School where his father was my English master. He was then in the lower forms and I was a prefect and about to go to Oxford. At that time he seemed to me to be just a mischievous schoolboy with the face of a Botticelli angel. I only got to know him seriously when I had come back to South Wales and he was already gaining a reputation as an up and coming young poet. He would return to Swansea after his forays into the London literary world, bringing with him an aura of contact with the great.

There was Edith Sitwell, a powerful poetic name in the early thirties. 'I've seen her,' said Dylan to me in triumph. 'A marvellous talking missal from the Middle Ages, and she positively gloats on my poems.' Apparently she did, for many

years after I was able to ask her
myself about her feelings for
Dylan. At that time she was a
sick woman, lying in bed in her
flat in Hampstead. I lived
not far away and my cellar
contained some
great white
burgundies, her
favourite wine.
I admit I used
to select a fine
bottle – say a
Montrachet or
a Meursault –
Genevrières – and
slip up to see her
against her doctor's orders.

But, as she said, doctors know nothing about the mind or the
heart. She proposed to leave this world with dignity and, if
possible, with a noble burgundy on her lips. She lay on her bed,
looking like a great medieval queen still receiving her courtiers
in her chamber of state, her hands encased in black gloves
extended upon a coverlet of red velvet. We talked of Dylan.

'How did he behave when he first met you?' I asked her.

'Beautifully,' and then she gave a slow smile. 'Beautifully,
but I've never seen him behave anything but beautifully with
me. He always behaved with me like a son with his mother.'

'Did he ever overstep the mark?'

'Well, one day he came to lunch with me. That was the only
time when I have seen him a little – well, perhaps a little over,
do you see? And he said, "I'm sorry to smell so awful, Edith,
it's Margate." "Ah," I said. "Yes, of course, my dear boy,
naturally it's Margate. I quite understand *that*."'

Dylan, frankly, was a little afraid of Edith Sitwell. He was
delighted to have her approval but was frightened of the

disaster of misbehaving in her presence. He need not have worried. She had the aristocratic gift of soothing over his wildest indiscretions with splendid tact. Others were not so kind or understanding. And now the Dylan I first knew has been swallowed by the legend; I have to keep reminding myself that the public Dylan was not the real Dylan.

I shall remember him as he was in his early twenties and the setting is always a pub in Swansea, after I had emerged from the valleys, and the talk flowed as copiously as the beer. Pubs were still pubs in those far-off days, and most of them were strictly male preserves. Their flavour, their atmosphere is now gone beyond recall. The brewers have engaged smart young architects and interior decorators to give them a facelift and drag them into our modern, mass-produced world. The air pulses with piped music and women seem to be the favourite clients, not men. In my day the only place for a woman in the ordinary pub was behind the bar. There were still old-style barmaids, amply proportioned and comforting, who knew how to dispense consolation as well as beer to their regulars. And the beer was still real beer, not the over-advertised, gaseous compounds poured out by modern breweries. The barmaids drew it 'from the wood', or pulled those beautifully decorated enamelled handles of the beer pumps, and the landlords were craftsmen who gained their reputations by the way they kept their wares in prime condition. By the standards of our new, 'progressive' society, the pubs of my youth were monstrously anti-social, even insanitary; but at least they had that elusive quality known as atmosphere – even if sometimes you could cut that atmosphere with a knife!

Such a pub was Number Ten in Mansel Street, Swansea, a favourite haunt of Dylan's and almost designed to be the proper setting for him. It had been reconstructed somewhere around 1900 in the Art Nouveau style. It had wonderful screens of fine woodwork dividing it up into discreet 'snugs', stained-glass windows and even an upstairs gallery, lined with drawings by Bert Thomas, the *Punch* artist who was Swansea's best known Thomas before Dylan. That upstairs gallery had a dashing, *fin de siècle* atmosphere about it. Here the ladies from the Swansea 'Emp', our music hall, could be tactfully entertained by their admirers. It was Swansea's nearest approach to Romano's. The central snug contained the pub's real sensation, the one thing that distinguished Number Ten from all other rival establishments – none other than a huge stuffed bear!

How on earth had this unlikely animal ever ended up in a Swansea pub? Dylan always maintained that the landlord had told him that it had been placed there by the first proprietor as a sure-fire attraction for his newly reconstructed inn. The bear had been well known in Swansea around 1900. His keeper used to bring him to High Street station to meet the trains. The bear would perform a dance and would end up embracing his keeper. The coins fairly showered down into the tin. After all, there are not many stations where the passengers are welcomed by a dancing bear. BR should take up the idea again. A dancing bear might solace the unhappy passengers as they listen to the inevitable announcement, 'The 4.30 train from Bristol Temple Meads will now be fifty minutes late. We regret any inconvenience caused to our passengers.'

Perhaps the bear also came to regret the inconvenience caused to him by his keeper, or he may have got irritated by the late arrival of the London express at Swansea. At any rate, the bear had obviously had enough, and showed his disapproval by crushing his keeper to death opposite Platform One. The poor bear was instantly shot, and the landlord of Number Ten, with his eye on advertisement, had it stuffed to become the main attraction in the central snug. Many a pint I drank with Dylan under the brooding presence of the bear.

Or more accurately, I ought to say, many a half pint – for I was now discovering that my body couldn't really take beer in bulk. Perhaps we are all born either natural beer drinkers or wine imbibers. Perhaps I ought to add whisky as well, for Scotland and Ireland remind us that beer and whisky can go together. Dylan certainly drank both with gusto, and, in my youth, I remember being introduced to the mysteries of the Glaswegian custom of the 'nip and chaser' – a whisky immediately followed by a pint of beer.

There were dangers in this practice not always obvious to the stranger to Glasgow. I was once taken by a journalist pal to a pub in the old district of the Gorbals – I believe it has now been swept away by the planners of the new, heartless, high-rise city. The bar was packed with men all taking 'the quickest road out of Glasgow'. It was savage drinking by leisurely South Wales standards, and all sorts of Jocks and Macs were hard at it knocking back their nips and chasers. Quietly a tiny little runt of a man, with a cloth cap pulled over his eyes, sneaked into the bar. My companion, who knew his way around, whispered to me, 'Watch this. He's Jimmy the Edger.'

The little man came softly up behind the booziest couple at the bar, who had obviously lost count of their drinking score.

Says Mac to Jock, 'Och, ye'll have anither,' and flings his arm around his pal's neck. A fatal move. Like greased lightning, little Jimmy has edged in, gulped down Mac's nip, and is away out through the door and on to the next crowded pub. All very wicked, but you were compelled to admire the sheer skill, the daring of it. Mac or Jock could have flattened little Jimmy the Edger with one swipe of their mighty hands if they had caught him. They never did. They were cumbersome drinking dinosaurs. The future lay with the quick-moving, quick-thinking edgers on the fringe of imbibing society.

There were no Dai the Edgers in Welsh pubs. In Number Ten we had undisturbed evenings of beer and talk before us. Dylan had a great gift for what I suppose we should call 'pub verse' – the rhymes came to him spontaneously as he downed his beer. I remember one evening when he maintained that, although we had a bear in our pub, life in Swansea would not be complete until the town had a resident vampire which could pay special attention to the Town Council and the Guildhall. And he chanted:

Councillors' jugulars suck I with glee;
Oh, for the blood of a scrumptious JP;
Tremble, ye Aldermen, Town Clerk beware,
As I hoover the veins of your succulent Mayor.

There were plenty of other verses, each one more outrageous than the last, although, of course, I never thought of writing them down. There would always be another day and the bank of verse was inexhaustible – or so we thought when we were young. But there was always one ingredient to the feast that went floating free and unrecorded into the smoke-laden atmosphere of Number Ten – Dylan's magnificent reciting voice. No poet ever did better justice to his own work.

Most poets should be prohibited from reciting their verse in public. I shall never forget the shock of hearing the great Yeats performing one of his poems – every word was drawn out like a piece of verbal elastic, every vowel fluted and caressed until the poet no longer seemed to be reciting but rather going into a trance. Auden was no great shakes at the reciting business and neither was Louis MacNiece. Roy Campbell was rather better, but he tended to boom away. Dylan had it just right, and I still cannot read a poem of his without hearing his organ voice rolling out from the printed page.

I do possess one complete Dylan 'pub poem', but only because he wrote it down himself, and I shall always associate it with the last time I ever drank a glass of beer. It happened in September 1943. I had just gone on an air raid over Berlin with the RAF – a terrifying nightmare in which I had escaped by the skin of my teeth when we shot down a night fighter attacking our Lancaster bomber just as he was about to do the same thing to us. When I came back, I beat the Pope himself in the business of thankfully kissing the tarmac.

After the broadcast, a well-known voice reached me on the phone. 'Hullo, hero. I'm in the last pub on the Kings Road.' It was Dylan and I guessed that he was in need of money. I immediately put £5 in my pocket and didn't regret a penny of it, for I was to be amply repaid. I naturally could not join Dylan immediately since I had to finish at the BBC and it must have been about 9 p.m. that I reached the pub. Dylan had employed the interval in writing a poem, but as time went by and the consumption of beer increased, the writing took on an ever increasing alcoholic slope. To read the last two lines you have to lie on the ground to counteract the angle. It didn't matter, because I knew, as I looked at it with non-alcoholic eyes in the morning, that at last I had got a genuine Dylan 'pub poem' on paper.

It was an uninhibited description of a Saturday night out in the little Cardigan port of New Quay, rich with fruity details which the local inhabitants would hardly recognise. It was a Welsh seaside community seen through the poet's beery eye, but do we detect in it a preview of *Under Milk Wood*?

Sooner than you can water milk or cry Amen
Darkness falls, psalming, over Cards, again;
Some lights go on; some men go out; some men slip in;
Some girls lie down, calling their beer-brown bulls to sin
And boom along their fishy fields; some elders stand
With thermoses and telescopes and spy the land
Where farmers plough by night and sailors rock and rise,
Tattooed with texts, between the Atlantic thighs
Of Mrs Rosser Tea and little Nell the Knock.
One pulls out *Pam in Paris* from his money sock.
One from the mothy darkness of his black back house
Drinks vinegar and paraffin and blinds a mouse.
One reads his cheque-book in the dark and eats fish-heads.
One creeps into the Cross Inn and fouls the beds.
One in the rubbered hedges rolls with a bald Liz

Who is old enough to be his mother – and she is!
Customers in the snug-bar by the gobgreen logs
Tell other customers what they do with dogs.
The chemist is performing an unnatural act
In the organ loft – and the lavatory is PACKED!

Monstrous and wildly divorced from reality, but a poet has a
right to fantasy and who wants reality, in any case, when you
are talking and drinking in a pub? Dylan had left out one of the
unique attractions of a lot of Welsh country pubs, the singing
at the bar. Wales must be the only country in the world where
people enjoy singing hymns in pubs, and where the traditional
toast at the local is *Pob llwyddiant i'r achos dirwestol!'* – 'All
success to the temperance cause!' It is happily celebrated with
draughts of strong ale. No irony intended. After all, most
country Welshmen have learnt their part singing in chapels and
they are grateful for the training. Success to the temperance
cause by all means, if it perfects your part singing.

Yes, Welsh pub singing was one of the pleasures of my Beer
Period, and it still flourishes, especially when the village's
male voice choir comes down to the local to refresh itself after
a practice night. Drop into the Fountain Inn at Pontardulais,
outside Swansea, and you are in for an unexpected evening's
delight. But, very early on, I made a disappointing discovery.
Pub singing only seems to flourish when the harmonious boys
are knocking back the wallop. It just doesn't go with wine
drinking. In France you consume wine in a café, or on those
delightful tables set out on the pavement before it. The sun is
shining, the pretty girls pass by before you, the animated young
men on the next table are surely artists about to leap into fame,
and the dignified gentleman with the trim white beard who is
reading *Le Temps* with a cognac before him is surely a
distinguished aristocrat, or at least a banker from the Bourse.
No, as you look around your café, you realise only too clearly
that the atmosphere is not conducive to hymn tunes sung in
chorus.

113

I expected better things when I first went to Italy as a young man but I had been wickedly deceived by the operatic composers. In Puccini's *La Bohème*, no one entered the Café Momus without trilling away at an aria. Every Verdi opera seemed to have a chorus of musical peasants, ready to burst out into a *brindisi*, or singing toast, at the drop of the conductor's baton. And it is well known – at least in opera – that in between holding up rich men for ransom, Sicilian bandits are distinctly partial to wine-drinking choruses in fruity harmony.

Unfortunately, when I went in search of all this splendid wine-inspired singing, I found that it had never left the operatic stage. The heirs to the Sicilian *banditi*, the Mafia, only 'sing' under the persuasive promptings of the Italian police. When it comes to happy singing over their wine, the Italians are a dead loss.

I did a little better when I first went to Germany. The Germans certainly burst out singing in 'taverns cool', but I have to admit that, again, it was beer not wine that inspired the singing. There was only one drawback about it. Those hearty Germanic drinking choruses all seemed to be heavily rehearsed. You felt that the singers had been carefully practising their choruses from official song books before they came rollicking into the bierkellers. I still longed for the off the cuff hymn-singing in Welsh country pubs. I would even order a half pint of beer again – yes, and drink it – if the Pontardulais Male Voice Choir would fill the bar with the rich harmonies of 'Bread of Heaven'. Indeed, I would join in with enthusiasm at the line, 'feed me till I want no more!'

It is high time that we return now to the Colonel in the café at Les Saintes-Maries-de-la-Mer. After all, it was his ordering a glass of beer that set me off on this diversion into my early world of ale, although I couldn't quite picture the Colonel being at home in a Welsh pub full of hymn-singers. But perhaps I misjudged him, for he suddenly revealed a side of his nature that I had never suspected, and a sense of humour which would have gone down well on the front in Blackpool. He finished off his beer and said to me, 'Ask this chap if he has got any postcards.' There were some rather tatty cards on a rack, showing the conventional tourist views of the Camargue, but, apparently, this was not exactly the sort of postcard the Colonel had in mind. He was a connoisseur of those rather pleasantly bawdy productions once associated with the name of Donald McGill and sold in all British seaside resorts. I actually met Donald McGill when he was approaching eighty and still producing his postcards – six new ones every year. He was a spry, white-haired little sparrow of a man, who lived, as he put it, 'near the business not the studio', in a Victorian villa in Streatham in the heart of London's southern suburbia. He was a keen supporter of Blackheath rugby club (keeping press-cuttings of all their games) and was therefore a beer drinker. All members of rugby clubs are so by long tradition.

This is certainly true of the rugby clubs of Wales, but Welsh rugby clubs in my day were radically different from English ones. In England rugby had a public school atmosphere about it. The shouts from the touchline were definitely of the 'Damn good show, chaps' variety. In a Welsh rugby match, the touchline shouting was almost a tribal ritual – the local rugby team, in the mining valleys, stood as a gesture of defiance against the surrounding squalor. The game was played with a harder edge on the field, although nothing could exceed the good-will in the club over the beer after the match.

I remember a rallying cry from the touchline at Ynysybwl. 'Rub their faces in the dirt, boys bach – but in a sporting fashion, of course.' Then there was the famous pre-match speech of a certain Welsh captain when his team was about to face the visiting All Blacks. His forwards were power-ful and great-hearted but hardly renowned for their intelligence – their leader was Dai Bungalow, so called because he had damn-all upstairs. The captain's oratory was fiery as befitted the occasion: 'Boys, I want you to go out there determined to win – yes, win I say, win at all costs. When you run on to the field you hold the honour of the valley in your hands. If you don't play your guts out, think of the fingers of shame that will be pointed at you on your way to chapel tomorrow. Go out there, boys, and crush them, yes, I say, crush them.' Then, thinking he might have overdone it, he hurriedly added, 'But don't forget I want a clean game, a sporting game. But don't forget also that you can play a cleaner and more sporting game against thirteen than against fifteen people.'

Nothing like this, I am sure, was ever heard at gentlemanly Blackheath; which heightens the contrast between the art of Donald McGill and his impeccable social background. When I met him he was a highly respectable widower, with a son and daughter.

I asked him, 'What do your family do when they pass a window full of your work?'

'Run like stags – all except my grandniece, who is proud of my work. She's at a most exclusive school for young ladies on the South Coast and she receives all the most fruity ones. Girls of thirteen these days know a damn sight more than I do.'

'Is your work vulgar?'

'Yes, of course it is – but not obscene, mind you. They loved it at the seaside. I seem to go with the sea air!'

'Have you ever lived at the seaside yourself?'

'What, Southend and that sort of thing? Good heavens, no. I can't understand what people see in the place, except my postcards, I'm thankful to say. Of course, Blackpool's our best seller. We can't go wrong there. North Wales is very good, too; in fact, anything north of the Thames is first class. But here's a funny thing, the Isle of Man wouldn't allow me to draw a clergyman; anything else – ladies with breasts like marrows are fine – but no clergymen. And who would have thought that I'd get fined at Cleethorpes – Cleethorpes of all places! Yes, they had me in court. "Wicked old white-haired grand-dad" – that was the headline in the local paper. You know, I felt quite disappointed that I didn't live up to it. Why, when you see Cleethorpes it looks like one of my postcards, now doesn't it? Cézanne, now. £100,000 for a canvas with all those strange women on it – that's vulgarity if you like!'

*

117

But how do you define vulgarity? What made the McGill type of vulgarity acceptable, even attractive? Surely it was because it was deeply rooted in the old English country tradition. The verses of the old folk-songs are full of it – before they were tactfully cleaned up by Victorian folk-song collectors. I am all the more certain of this because I was lucky enough to know one of the last genuine folk-singers. Needless to say, it was during my Beer Period. English folk-song was washed happily along entirely by beer.

Phil Tanner lived in Gower; that delectable and still largely unspoilt peninsula that stretches westwards from the industrial port of Swansea in South Wales in eighteen miles of lonely moorlands and sandy bays backed by glittering limestone cliffs. Gower has been entirely English-speaking for over 700 years, for the Normans swept out all the Welsh in the twelfth century. When I met him, Phil was already well known as the Gower Nightingale – a nobly bearded patriarch with a wicked twinkle in his eye and a fund of songs and stories, and always accompanied by a friendly sheepdog  that thrust a cool nose into our hot hands. Phil always sat in summer on his bench outside the King's Head in Llangennith, tactfully supplied with ale by his admirers, and ready to bring us all the flavour of that unspoilt Gower in the last days of Queen Victoria.

His songs were his real glory. He had picked them up from

all sorts of sources, music halls, travelling tinkers, songs handed down from the distant past. He would clear his throat, down his glass, call 'Order, order, gentlemen, singing is a serious matter,' and ring out the first verse while the dog would whimper in protest.

It was back in Tipperary I was born when I was young
And that's the reason that I've got the blarney on my tongue.
I was the image of my daddy, even the doctor did allow,
And the girls all came to kiss me – Oh, I wish they'd do it now!

(Down bitch, drat her, what's the matter with her. She was musical enough as a puppy.) We joyfully joined in the chorus.

How I wish they'd do it now. How I wish they'd do it now.
They'd tickle me down all over – Oh, I *wish* they'd do it now!

Then there were what Phil called his 'naughty ones'. Looking back on it, how innocent they all were, those 'naughty ones' of Phil's! Our permissive society wouldn't have turned a hair as Phil, glancing around hurriedly to make sure no ladies were present, gave us the Gower Toast:

> Here's to the maiden bright with honour;
> Many's the time I've lain upon her.
> I've done it standing; I've done it lying,
> And if I'd wings [*whistle*] I'd had done it flying!

Innocent bawdry from both Phil Tanner and Donald McGill has been totally overtaken by the pornographic flood that has now engulfed film, radio and TV. I look back on those unsophisticated days with nostalgia, but, in August 1944, how was I to explain to our café proprietor in Les Saintes-Maries in the Camargue the subtle differences we have just been discussing between the permissible and the non-permissible? Especially when it came to picture postcards at the seaside! I tried a tentative sentence: '*Mon ami desire quelque chose legèrement pornographique.*' The French language has no room for the friendly vagueness of English. French is logical and precise and has no method of expressing anything 'lightly pornographic'. Our café owner said firmly, 'Our café is in the shadow of the church and I am a Catholic. Such goods are only sold quietly by the chemist, who is an atheist and a Republican.' It was time for us to leave and return to the war. There, at least, everything was in black and white.

We drove back through the deserted Camargue under the bright sun. At Orange, in the shadow of the Roman amphitheatre, I had my last drink with the Colonel – his was still a beer, but mine was a glass of Tavel. We were leaving the indifferent wines of Provence and approaching the far more serious vineyards of the Côtes-du-Rhône. I was sorry to say good-bye to the Colonel. He had been a good companion, but he represented my Beer Period. As he said to me, rather wistfully, as we parted: 'Well, good-bye, old chap. Don't suppose we'll meet again. This war has made me feel that I'm what you might call a Dying Type.' I watched the Dying Type get into his jeep, firmly British to the end as he drove off down the left-hand side of the road.

I went north to the sound of the guns and a link-up with my new wine guru, the young vintage-knowledgeable French lieutenant who I had met at Les Baux. I looked at the intriguing wine names that lay ahead of us on the map – wines I had read about but not yet tasted. Were the Hermitage growths still good? What about Côte Rôtie? I resolved to complete my education as I brought freedom to these illustrious gastronomic strongpoints.

CHAPTER FIVE

Burgundian Glory

The Rhône is a noble stream. Today it may have been heavily harnessed by *barrages* and power stations, but in 1944 it still gave an impression of untamed power inherited from its wild source among the glaciers of the Alps. It flowed swiftly under the hills near Valance, terraced by vineyards. I put up at a friendly little hotel just outside the town, for I felt in need of some soul-searching over a good bottle before I rejoined the French army. Just as I had relived my Beer Period in the Camargue, so here, slightly withdrawn from the battle, with the vineyards all around me

and the Rhône bright in the sunlight at the end of the hotel garden, I had my chance to look back on the way I had come to the world of wine.

In 1936 I joined the Welsh Region of the BBC as an Outside Broadcast Assistant at the then princely salary of £250 a year. Frankly it was high time that I moved out of my work among the unemployed before the government auditors caught up with me. I was confirmed in my decision by a visit to a certain club to which I had given the statutory grant of £25. The club was housed in a deserted warehouse and I had hoped to find it a hive of activity, with shoe repairing in full swing, lectures on cultural subjects and tools being prepared for digging on the allotments to supplement the dole. The ground floor was strangely deserted and so was the first; but up on the second floor I found the whole membership bunched around a wide window. The chairman spun round and then advanced on me with a slightly spurious welcome.

'Mr Vaughan-Thomas, I'm delighted to see you. Only last night the committee passed a resolution inviting you to come and meet us.'

'What's going on?'

'Well, to tell you the truth – no, to tell you the honest truth – we can see the local greyhound track from here.'

A shudder went through me. Government money punted on the dogs! How would I explain *that* away? The chairman rushed to reassure me. 'We're on a winner, and when he romps home, we'll have double the money to do all the things that will delight your heart – we'll even have classes on economic history under the Rev. Will Rees "Elevated Thought". It's in the bag.'

'Yes, but suppose things go wrong?'

'Impossible. Dai Bach's brother is letting them out of the trap.' Then came the now inevitable assumption. 'In any case, Mr Thomas, we know that we can rely on you.'

But could I dare perform yet another feat of financial leger-demain? In my pocket I carried an advertisement for a post in the BBC. I sent off my application that very night. It was, I am convinced, a near-run thing, but at last I was safe in the Corporation's arms. I could now leave beer for wine – but here's a pretty paradox. How could I enter the world of wine through the portals of an organisation as sternly devoted to teetotalism as any Welsh chapel? When I joined it, the BBC was still under the iron rule of that strange martinet of culture, Sir John – later Lord – Reith. Joining the Corporation in the 1930s was rather like becoming a novice in a Jesuit seminary. You were dedicated to the improvement of the masses. As Sir John put it to me when he received me in his vast office on the third floor of the still new Broadcasting House, looking out over London like the captain on the bridge of a great liner loaded with high-minded and culture-dedicated passengers,

'Welcome aboard,' and, after an outline of the standard of conduct he expected from a new member of the Noble Order of Sanctified Broadcasters, he added his final word, 'Never forget that the BBC is not an organ of mere entertainment.'

I had, however, joined a department that came perilously close to 'mere entertainment'. In Outside Broadcasts, we dealt with commentaries on great occasions but also with sport, from racing to boxing. The Director General cast anxious eyes on us, for we were certainly exposed to temptation. His worst fears were justified when that brilliant commentator, the late Commander Thomas Woodroofe, succeeded, to vast popular delight, in 'lighting up the fleet' on the occasion of the Coronation Review of the Fleet in 1936.

It was not exactly Tommy's fault. He had gone back to his old ship, HMS *Nelson*, to do his commentary. He had, unfortunately, done himself rather well with old pals in the

wardroom. As he climbed up to his commentary point in the fighting top, the sea air had its inevitable effect. The sober, steady voice of Stuart Hibberd came over to Portsmouth and the not so steady and distinctly unsober voice of Tommy Woodroofe took up the story.

'The fleet's lit up . . . dozens of fairy lights . . .they're gone . . . there's nothing between me but sea and sky . . .' Again and again the amazed listeners were assured that the fleet, like the commentator, was completely 'lit up', until the announcer tactfully faded out the whole fantasia.

I had an appointment to meet Tommy the next day and had come up by the night train. I had therefore missed the whole broadcast but as I walked through the quiet streets from Paddington I found London plastered with mysterious posters. 'The Fleet's Lit Up,' they proclaimed. 'Remarkable Description by Naval Commander.' 'Fairy Lights over the Royal Navy!' When I entered Broadcasting House I found an atmosphere of hushed disaster, as if a rich uncle had suddenly died and was found to be bankrupt. I passed Recorded Programmes. 'What's up?' I asked. 'Didn't you hear it?' And they lured me into a cubicle where I had a private audition of the first earthquake to crack the solid structure of the British Broadcasting Corporation.

Clearly my arrangements for meeting Tommy were off. I left the stricken purlieus of BH and walked down Upper Regent Street. Coming towards me was a well-known bowler-hatted figure with an elegantly rolled umbrella. By heavens, it was Tommy himself. He had been more or less flung ashore from HMS *Nelson* and now he was coming in to face the music. He stopped and gave me a brave, disarming grin.

'What will you do, Tommy?' I asked.

'Well, you know what I always say. Never look back, never apologise, keep on talking. I'll have to look back now, but by heavens, I'm going to keep on talking.'

'Good luck,' I said.

'I'll need it,' he replied. He squared his shoulders, set his bowler at a jaunty angle (popularised by Admiral Beatty), put his umbrella to his shoulder and stepped boldly toward the wrath of Sir John Reith awaiting him on the third floor of Broadcasting House.

I regarded it as a pretty piece of irony that, on the very same day that Tommy was facing the Wrath of Reith on the third floor of a stricken Broadcasting House, I was on floor two having my first meeting with the man who was to lead me into the Paths of Righteousness as far as wine was concerned. Dear André Simon had not come to BH that momentous morning to talk about wine. Under the Reith regime that would have been unthinkable. In fact no programme dealing with wine was broadcast by the BBC until the early 1950s, after the war,

when I had the good fortune to accompany André and Laurence Gilliam, Head of Feature Programmes, to Bordeaux. There was much head-shaking among the programme planners before we set off. They gave us a final counsel, as if they were still looking over their shoulder in case Lord Reith appeared. 'Stick to the facts and for heaven's sake, don't make too much about wine drinking as a pleasure.' But that was exactly what André conveyed to me on our first meeting. Wine was a civilised pleasure which had its roots deep in the old culture of Europe.

André was a powerful fountainhead of quotations about the delights of wine. This was the occasion when he first decided that my Welsh name was too complicated and appropriately christened me 'Vineyard' Vaughan-Thomas. Then he powerfully impressed me at lunch in the Écu de France by sending back a bottle of burgundy as being unworthy of its place of origin. What knowledge, what authority, what courage!

I am a vinous coward and never dare to reject a bottle in a restaurant once it has been opened. There was a time – long since passed – when socially climbing young men would impress their girl friends by tasting their first glass and then sternly declaring, 'Waiter, this wine is corked.' Now, wine is 'corked' when air has got into the bottle and the taste and smell are very nasty indeed. Corked wine is rare. I may have been lucky, but in a long career of wine-drinking in restaurants I have

never been served a corked wine. The old head waiters had their own way of dealing with these egregious young gentlemen. They immediately agreed with the verdict, whisked the wine away, and a fresh waiter reappeared with the same wine, wrapped in a different serviette. The wine was poured out again, the brash young man raised the glass to his lips and said gravely, 'Yes, my man, that's more like it.'

The little ritual gave satisfaction all round, but it early taught me a lesson. If you want to get the best out of wine, it's worth while giving a little time to studying it. After all, you are going to drink a lot of it in the course of your life. And, by the way, has anyone calculated the actual volume of wine the average wine-drinker consumes in his lifetime? No, on second thoughts, I don't want to know my statistical wine intake. I've reached a pleasant old age. I have drunk my wine in moderation and with respect. It has given me innocent pleasure all my life, and, for that, I must thank André Simon.

On that first lunch, he talked with enthusiasm about the club he had formed a few years before with A. J. A. Symons, in honour of that great wine expert and authority on Civilised Drinking, Professor George Saintsbury. Saintsbury had published his classic *Notes on a Cellar Book*, an account of his wine purchases over three decades together with his judgement on the vintages, which had immediately become a wine-lovers' classic. In these days, when wine books rival cookery books and books about Royalty in popularity with publishers, and lavishly produced and authoritative volumes like Hugh Johnston's *Atlas of Wine* are readily available to anyone taking the first steps in wine appreciation, it is hard to recall how few and far between were wine books in the thirties. They were, however, of high literary quality. I have happy memories of Maurice Healey's *Stay Me with Flagons*. 'Maurice was a teetotaller until I met him,' said André. An Irish teetotaller! It seems a contradiction in terms. There were the elegant volumes of H. Warner Allen, compact with classical learning, and P. Morton Shand on the *Wines of France*. But Professor Saintsbury, somehow, outdid them all.

What wines he drank – all pre-phylloxera – and with what relish he described them! He didn't pull his punches – as witness his opinion of Lacryma Christi – but, then, he was a High Tory with a wicked command of invective. The proposed Saintsbury Club would unite literary wine-lovers with distinguished wine merchants and shippers. It would meet twice a year, and consume and judge the to be carefully laid down wines in Vintner's Hall in London. All that was now needed was the blessing of the Professor. The club founders wrote to the old gentleman, who was now living in retirement in the Royal Crescent in Bath. They invited him to lunch, but they

received a characteristic answer. He declared – as far as André could decipher his appalling writing – that he would not lunch with them, or anyone else, anyhow, anywhere, at any time. There was nothing for it but to form the Saintsbury Club, not

with the blessing but with the muttered curses of
the patron saint. Happily the Club still flourishes
and I had the honour of being elected to it after
the war. At our last meeting we sampled the
'45 Château Latour. It was magnificent, but as I
lifted my glass to my lips I murmured a little
prayer of thanks, not to the irrascible Professor
Saintsbury, but to kindly André Simon, who so
pleasantly opened the door for me into the
world of wine.

Looking back on it, the wines we studied in the thirties all
came from classic wine areas – claret, burgundy, hock, port,
sherry, Madeira and Cognac. These were the names with
which we strove to become familiar. There must have been
merchants who imported Loire wines or even Hungarian
wines, but I never patronised them. The Beaujolais Nouveau
business had not burst on the British drinking scene at the time
I was learning my wine. Frankly I am no fan of this over-
publicised PR racket. But I did regret I hadn't really studied
the Rhône wines before I found myself campaigning among
them. I had read all about them, of course, and names like
Châteauneuf-du-Pape seemed as romantic
as Lacryma Christi. Thankfully Châteauneuf
tasted far better when I at last drank it as I
entered the town in the Liberation.
There were now other Rhône wines ahead
of me waiting to be sampled, above all,
I suddenly remembered, Saint-Péray
itself, the product of the little town I was
going to liberate in the morning. I must
admit that my great expectations about

Saint-Péray were not derived from the experts like P. Morton Shand, but from a poet, none other than that rather prim Victorian, Arthur Hugh Clough. I suppose that he is only remembered now as the author of those verses beginning with the stern admonition: 'Say not the struggle naught availeth', and ending with the line quoted by Churchill to cheer us up in one of the darkest days of the war: 'And westwards, lo, the land is bright'. That land was America, which had just come into the war and thus given us hope of ultimate victory.

I lapped up the quotation at the time, but I couldn't take Arthur Hugh totally seriously as a prophet because I had already unearthed some poems of his which showed him to be the possessor of a pretty vein of ironic wit. He was also a bon vivant, who wrote this wry piece about rich men dining:

> Your Chablis is acid, away with the Hock,
> Give me the pure juice of the purple Médoc:
> Saint-Péray is exquisite, but, if you please,
> Some Burgundy just before tasting the cheese.
> How pleasant it is to have money, heigh-ho!
> How pleasant it is to have money.

The sting in the tail comes in the next verse:

> As for that, pass the bottle and d—m the expense,
> I've seen it observed by a person of sense,
> That the labouring classes could scarce live a day,
> If people like us didn't eat, drink, and pay.
> So useful it is to have money, heigh-ho!
> So useful it is to have money.

Useful indeed! Karl Marx would have taken two turgid chapters of *Das Kapital* to say the same thing.

But it was that clear-cut statement, 'Saint-Péray is exquisite' that stuck in my memory. In mid-Victorian days it was clearly regarded as worthy to stand side by side with the great clarets and burgundies. I naturally ordered a bottle immediately I came to my inn. I drank it with Clough's eulogy in my mind, which was perhaps a little unfair. It was a white wine that was offered to me – good and enjoyable but certainly not exquisite. My host assured me that Saint-Péray had been one of the favourite wines of Wagner, but as I am no Wagnerian fan – I once suffered days at Covent Garden coping with the *Ring* – this was not exactly a recommendation. Obviously something had happened to this wine since the mid-nineteenth century. It had met its *Götterdämmerung*. The solution of the mystery was simple. Poor Saint-Péray was one of those vintages that had never fully recovered from the sad affair of the phylloxera.

The phylloxera was a wicked little bug that arrived from North America in the late 1860s, and happily gnawed its way for the next decade through every vine in sight. It wasn't only the French vines which were affected. Eventually this unattractive louse invaded every vineyard in the world. Were the pleasures of wine about to be swept off the face of the earth? But just as the plague came from North America, so did the remedy. The triumphant teetotal hymns in Welsh chapels died away in disappointment when it was discovered that you could double-cross the phylloxera bug if you grafted the fine French stocks on to North American roots. Vintage wine breathed again.

But all through the years between the wars, when I was taking my first tentative steps in wine, there were plenty of old codgers left who took a malicious pleasure – just as you were praising some splendid wine – in puncturing your self-esteem by remarking, 'Not a patch on the pre-phylloxera Latour, young man.'

André Simon had naturally drunk extensively of both pre- and post-phylloxera offerings, and I have a feeling that, in his heart of hearts, he admitted the superiority of the great pre-phylloxera vintages. They had more staying power, and André relished the ripeness that came with vigorous old age. He it was who introduced me to the charms of old vintage champagne, in which the last bubbles slowly float up through a golden haze, like one of the *grandes horizontales* of the *belle époque*, a Cloe de Mèrode of wine, making a gallant last effort to please a rich but aged lover.

So much more elegant than those barbarians of the motor races who spray magnums of vintage Krug or Pol Roger over themselves like cheap scent, in celebration of noisy victory. I prefer to let history creep up on me as I savour the last drop of an old and rare wine.

I have been lucky to taste some few pre-phylloxera bottles myself. The oldest was a Madeira – perhaps the longest-living wine in the world. I am sometimes tempted to compare these rare, long-living bottles to those equally remarkable old men – Manny Shinwell is one who has passed his hundred – who defy all natural law, and grow steadily more interesting as they grow older and older.

Such a splendid octogenarian was the late Frank Lloyd Wright, the great American architect and one of the founding fathers of the modern movement, who I had a chance of interviewing for television when he came to Wales after the war. He was very proud of his Welsh origins, and when he was well into his eighties he accepted a Honorary Degree from the University of Wales. The ceremony took place in Bangor, but in those early days of television, the BBC could not get a line further west than Rhyl, on the North Wales coast. The great man was persuaded to make the journey to this somewhat brash seaside resort, where we put him up for the night in the Queen's Hotel, a marvellous bit of Edwardian architectural fretwork but hardly the most appropriate resting place for a master of the modern movement. I must say that, when he came into our temporary studio accompanied by his 25-year-old secretary, he looked as if he was going to crumble before my very eyes. I was sure that he was not long for this world and no doubt out viewers felt the same.

I therefore conducted the interview on reverential lines, and at the end, as tactfully as I could, asked if he had made arrangements to pass on his knowledge and inspiration to coming generations. He gave me a slightly old-fashioned look as he replied, 'Yes, sir, I have a fine group of young men around me and we've a great deal of work ahead – the extension of the Guggenheim Museum and the Mile High project. And if the Lord spares me .l. .' Here I looked suitably reverent and pious as he continued, 'Yes, sir, if the Lord spares me (a slight pause and then in a ringing voice), if he spares me, I reckon we'll clean up a cool three million daolars.' No question about the strength of the wine still held in that remarkable old bottle!

*

I had no further time for reflection on ancient wines, for, at St Péray, I linked up again with my wine-knowledgeable young French lieutenant and his scout group. A good move, for we were now pushing the Germans out of some of the finest of the Rhône vineyards. We cleared them away from the remarkable hill of Hermitage, north of Valence. We could hardly miss it, for the slopes rise steeply from the road, railway and river, all terraced with the names of the proud proprietors displayed on the white walls.

We reached Vienne, the largest town in an area of remarkable wine. Just across the river is Château-Grillet which I had already drunk with my young French lieutenant at Les Baux, and Côte Rôtie – the 'noble breed' as P. Morton Shand calls it. Shand fairly lets himself go in learning and adjectives when he comes to Côte Rôtie. It was apparently praised by Plutarch, Martial and Pliny, and all these 'wines of Vienne' had

a ready market in Rome because of their 'pitchy' quality. This hardly describes their taste today. Morton Shand claims that it is the 'very antithesis of the ripe-raspberry flavour and violet-scented bouquet' that characterises the best Côte Rôtie now. My French lieutenant, with his flair for good wine and good living, took care to be the first into Vienne where, as far as he was concerned, the chief treasure was the noble Restaurant du Pyramid, kept by Monsieur Point.

The master chef welcomed us with open arms and bottles, for he had made his restaurant a secret centre of the Resistance during the war years, and many an indiscreet conversation by German generals reached Allied intelligence after they had sampled M. Point's cooking. The Côte Rôtie he offered us certainly lived up to Morton Shand's euconium, but when, at last, we tore ourselves away from M. Point's patriotic hospitality and crossed the river to the vineyards, I was surprised to see how small so many of them were – especially the more famous ones. No wonder great Côte Rôtie is rare, and it set me wondering how some well-known names of certain French wines are so plentiful on the English market. Is there a vinous law of expansion by which the area under vines increases in proportion to the publicity obtained?

Perish the unworthy thought, for we were now approaching Lyons, and for the moment wine had to take second place in my war reporting. A great city in the delirium of liberation is no place for the study of fine wine. I suspended my vinous education and rejoiced in the joyful uproar of the crowded streets until, in the middle of the celebrations, it suddenly struck me that it was my duty to catch up with all that was happening in the rest of the war. Reluctantly I admitted to myself that there were important military objectives other than great vineyards. Where had Eisenhower's armies got to in their race across northern France? Was the Russian steam-roller approaching the German borders on the eastern front? In truth, when you are absorbed in the excitement of your own small section of the war, you forget that the rest of the world, to a greater or lesser degree, is caught up in the struggle. One man's war is totally different from another's, yet everyone may be convinced that his own particular section is playing a vital part in final victory.

I had a curious reminder of this when I came across the diary of the Bow Street Home Guard after the war. It was a wonderful glimpse of what was happening in the rural parts of my native Wales while I may have been flying in a bomber over Berlin or cowering in a slit trench on the Anzio beachhead or even drinking my way up the Rhône valley.

Bow Street is a straggling village just north of Aberystwyth in west Wales and the Home Guard was embodied on 11 November 1940, when the village felt itself threatened by a possible German invasion in Cardigan Bay. The gallant

volunteers formed up outside the Memorial Hall and marched out to war as the women and children ran besides them shouting, 'Come back safe!' They swung smartly down the road and turned sharp left into the strongpoint they were to hold with grim determination throughout the rest of the war – the ladies waiting-room at Bow Street station! That evening they made their first important entry in their War Diary (which, I am glad to say, has been carefully preserved by the railway authorities). The state of the defences was carefully noted: 'Equipment checked 8.30.p.m. 1 teapot, 1 kettle, 1 dartboard, 3 darts, 1 shotgun, 5 rounds, pack of cards missing. All quiet.'

Conditions got tough during the grim winter of 1940. In December came the disconcerting report, 'Hole burnt in blanket', but the defences remained at full strength: '29 January 1941. Equipment checked at 8.30 p.m. 1 teapot (spout broken), 1 kettle, 1 dartboard, 3 darts, 2 mugs, 2 shotguns, pack of cards (joker missing). All quiet.' Then as Hitler's Panzer divisions crashed through Russia, the Bow Street Home Guard also faced a grim crisis: '2 July 1941. When I came on duty this morning the guards had been throwing lumps of bread on the floor. Soon this place will be overrun by mice.'

The war strain deepened. By August conditions had become desperate: '12 August 1941. Password "Chips and Beans". Can't sleep: Evans is pushing me out of bed.' But at last – at the very time I was liberating Lyons – action and danger were at hand in Bow Street. '12 September 1944. Alerted guard. Police reported suspicious character on road to Aberystwyth. Person intercepted and examined. He declared he was on a mission of an amorous nature. Allowed to proceed. Patrol continued up road and found freshly painted inscription, "To Hell with Churchill. Freedom for Wales!"' At last the enemy had attacked.

But steadily, through 1944, the ladies' waiting-room on the down platform was strengthened, the guns available went up to three, and two teapots and a new pack of cards were added to the defences. So bravely checking their darts, clinging to their burnt blankets and shouting 'Chips and Beans' to each other through the lonely watches of the night, the Home Guard of Bow Street saw out the war. Or did they? From the diary it seems unclear that they have yet realised that the war has ended, for the last entry simply reads, with commendable caution, 'All Clear – presumably!'

Back in the Rhône valley, I had no doubt that it was 'All Clear' ahead. After the fall of Lyons, the Germans pulled back at a steady rate, with an occasional stand by the rear-guard to make sure that we did not outflank them. I was now on my own. The Colonel had disappeared back to England and my French lieutenant had also disappeared – I suspect in search of his family. I didn't blame him. He hadn't heard of his family for three years and I'm sure that he wangled a few days' compassionate leave at Lyons. I could picture the family reunion and the array of splendid bottles on the table. I admit that I missed both the Colonel and my wine guru. They might have prevented me from nearly coming to grief as I tried to keep up with the French army.

I was driving on a dusty white road on the outskirts of Lyons and failed to notice that the surroundings were suspiciously quiet all of a sudden. There came a strange, whistling sound, a sharp crump and a chunk of the road suddenly shot up in a white fountain before me. I was an old soldier by this time. My mind immediately flicked on the warning light, 'German tank. Get the hell out of this.' I swung through a pair of elaborate iron gates on my right. I found myself – of all places in a war – in a large cemetery. I didn't stop to think. There was a vast memorial tomb in front of me, good, solid cover. I was out of the jeep in a flash and crouched down behind an elaborate piece of sculpture with a carved angel holding a stone wreath over my head. I was a curiously unmilitary figure as I huddled closer to the memorial and a machine gun started to chip off the fingers of an angel on the next tomb.

'Damn it,' I muttered to myself, 'what an insult, after all I've escaped from so far, to be wounded in a French cemetery with all those great vineyards ahead!' I crawled still closer to the most solid part of the surrounding angels and waited. Then I remembered the advice given to me by a tough old sergeant in the Irish Guards when we were lying together in a damp ditch on the Anzio beachhead. A hard-pressed unit on our right, shelled beyond endurance, held up their hands in surrender. Night was falling, the Germans were edging around behind us. The sergeant took in the situation at a glance. 'We've got to get out of this.' I sprang up to run when the sergeant hurriedly pulled me down. 'Now, lad, take a tip! Whenever you feel like running – and we'll sure be moving in a minute – always count five slowly, however frightened you are. Then it's ten to one that the man to the right or left of you will run first. Then you can run after him, shouting, "Come back. Face the enemy. Stand. Rally round me." No one will, of course, but you've covered yourself with glory. You'll get the medal and you'll get safely out of the mess as well. Now, count five, and follow me.'

I followed that sergeant's advice as I crouched in my cemetery hiding place. The firing died down into an odd crackle away to the right. I was still in one piece and I resolved to count not just to five, but for half an hour. No sense in trying my luck too far. I even started to look at the inscriptions on the nearby memorial stones. I confess I have a secret pleasure in wandering around churchyards. There's nothing macabre about this. Country churchyards in Britain can be places of tranquil beauty with all the past history of the parish for three hundred years spread before you. And the inscriptions on the tombstones can be an added pleasure. In a Welsh churchyard the other day I came across a delightful verse, which I translate:

Deep in this grave lies lazy Dai,
Waiting the last Great Trump on high.
If he's as fond of his grave as he was of his bed,
He'll be the last man up when that roll-call's said.

French graveyards don't lend themselves to such esoteric pleasures. The tombstones are too florid and elaborate, and at the beginning of the century the horrid practice grew up of placing a photograph of the deceased in a cast-iron frame behind glass in the centre of the tombstone. I looked at these curious and slightly faded objects and couldn't help noticing how plump these solid Lyonnais citizens all were; and everyone leaving this life in his late fifties! There was no doubt about it – their photographs showed that they had eaten not wisely but too well. They were martyrs to the glories of French gastronomy.

I plucked up courage again. I, at least, was still in the position to eat, drink and be merry, and what opportunities now lay ahead! The Beaujolais! If there ever was a part of France which deserved the Biblical accolade of being a land flowing with milk and honey, and with wine as well, this was it. The vineyards start on the rich plain and extend, in their carefully tended rows, up to the encircling hills. An air of good living laps the little towns and villages in a rich contentment.

This is the countryside of Gabriel Chevalier's novel *Cloche-merle*, that epic history of the battle over a public lavatory in a little town of the Beaujolais, which we read with chuckling pleasure just before the war. It was suffused with kindly laughter over human frailty, flavoured by the generous eating and drinking of a society which knew how to get through the trials of life in the easiest way possible.

The food of the Beaujolais stands side by side with the wine in *Clochemerle*. I read of the succulent *poulets* of Bresse, the *quenelles de brochet* from the pike of the Saône, the frogs' legs and the beef that is reputed to be the best in France. The Beaujolais is, after all, the home of the Charollais cattle, and, in recent years, we have been only too glad to import Charollais on to British pastures. All this, and wine too! I smacked my lips in anticipation.

As I write that last sentence, I hurriedly recall that I have already been somewhat scornful about one aspect of the Beaujolais wine world – the race to get the first wine of the year on to the market. It's great fun, I agree, but the fun obscures the other splendid wines the area produces – Moulin-à-Vent, Juliénas, Fleurie and the rest of them. These are the vintages that really give the Beaujolais and the Mâconnais their renown. And the *primeur* business has made the very name of Beaujolais so popular in Britain that the supply seems to have mysteriously increased with the demand. It has, in the tactful French term, been 'stretched'. In other words, some of the Beaujolais we happily consume in this country has, to quote old Wordsworth, 'had elsewhere its setting, and cometh from afar'. Again, I suppose I ought to be indulgent to the Beaujolais publicity business because it has its roots in the long history of the wine. The Beaujolais wine-growers, from the very begin-ning, have been masters of PR, and the wine first hit the headlines back in the seventeenth century, by a brilliant piece of advertising which would have done credit to many a modern practitioner of the art.

The story goes that, in 1660, a vine-dresser named Claude

Brosse – a man as tall as he was enterprising – set off from Mâcon to try and interest some of the great lords of the French court in his wine. He attended mass at Versailles, and the King was disgusted to see what he thought was a man standing up when the mass had reached a point when he should have been reverently kneeling down. He sent his guards to arrest the blasphemer, but they returned to the King to report that the man had actually been kneeling, but even in that position he overtopped everyone in the congregation. The King immediately wanted to see the giant. Claude Brosse appeared before him in his wine-grower's costume, and bowed deeply to the King. Louis enquired what he was doing in Versailles. Brosse

explained that he had come in the hope of interesting some great lord in his wine. 'I am the greatest lord here,' smiled the King. 'Let me try it.' He did so, pronounced it excellent and the courtiers immediately tumbled over themselves to order it in quantities. Brosse's fortune was made, and with it, the fortunes of the Beaujolais as a whole. Perhaps we ought to regard Brosse as the first organiser of the race to bring the Beaujolais nouveau to market even though he carried his wine to Paris in ox-waggons. The Italians may have the best names for wines but the French have the best stories!

So this land of vinous joy lay ready to welcome me – I can speak of this welcome in personal terms, for the French forces were naturally occupied in driving the Germans up the main roads and had no time to send out units bearing the message of liberation to all the small towns and villages scattered among the vineyards in the hills. I felt that this was a task I should undertake myself for the honour, not only of France, but of Britain as well. For the next few days I was the harbinger of freedom to the more scattered parts of the Beaujolais. The process almost became a ritual, but a ritual of pure pleasure. First came the rush through the excited crowds to the *Mairie*, then the welcome on the *Mairie* steps by the mayor in the rich sash of his office and my speech, in recklessly ungrammatical but florid French, to the flag-waving and bottle-offering citizens. I can still remember some of the phrases of my standardised speech from the Mairie steps:

'*Votre chère ville, dont le renomée remont à l'epoche gallo-romain* . . . Your beautiful town, whose fame goes back to the age of the Celts and the Romans . . . Your wine, enjoyed by the great men of history, from Pliny to the *Roi Soleil* himself . . . Shall I compare it to a beautiful woman, who gains in charm as she gains in years . . .'

How the sentences tumbled out, and how brilliant they sounded – at the time!

There was one little town, however, where my standard liberation speech didn't make its usual impression. I had reached the point where I compared the local wine to a beautiful woman, when the ranks of the crowd parted and a large, imposing lady appeared, followed by five charming girls. She looked like a majestic battleship, leading five little destroyers in her wake. She was the *madame* from the local *maison de tolérance*. She embraced me in a cloud of scent. The crowd cheered, and as I emerged from her ample bust, she pointed to her young ladies and beamed, 'For you, the brave liberator.' I drew back in consternation, but Madame hastened to reassure me. 'Have no fear. My ladies have been patriotic. Only the one with cross-eyes slept with the Germans.' My *pudeur britannique*

prevailed. I hurriedly explained that I had to follow the French advance immediately and headed for fresh and less dangerous pastures of liberation.

How history repeats itself! I thought I would never again need the standardised speech, but fifteen years after the war I found myself at it again. This time Britain was happily occupied in giving its empire away. The freedom ceremonies came so thick and fast across the African continent that I almost stylised the commentary.

'Now midnight strikes. The guns boom out in salute. The Union Jack is hauled slowly down from the masthead, and, in its place, against the star-lit African sky rises the hopeful new flag of . . .' Heavens, where were we now? What on earth was the name of this happy new country? A quick glance at the order of ceremony, and I gasped out the new title in the nick of time. British prestige was saved!

That French adventure also set me thinking how widely different are the standards of sexual morality around the world. I'm talking about the standards of 1944, of course. Today, all has changed. The *pudeur britannique* no longer exists. If you want to find stricter standards of sexual conduct, according to the accepted rules of society, you have to turn to Africa. At the time I was making my second set of standardised speeches of liberation, I found myself in Ghana. To celebrate the advent of freedom the new rulers decided to stage the first beauty contest ever held in Africa.

My sympathies went out to them as they grappled with unfamiliar problems. A beauty competition is a fantastic Western ritual, whose rules are very difficult to explain to the average Westerner, leave alone to the inhabitants of Accra. Madame and her five little destroyers from the Beaujolais would have been sternly shown the door. It was therefore not surprising that there were some unusual comments when the entrants arrived at the Community Centre in a bus marked 'Mass Education'. There had been six hundred applicants and now here were the finalists, competing for a free trip to

London and the battle for the title of Miss World. Other countries in Africa had their eyes on the title, however. The local press had that very morning warned Ghana of the dangers of competition: 'Six Dakar Cuties Couched by French Experts for World Honour.'

When we arrived at the Community Centre we found it besieged by amorous wolves who kept up a running fire of comment as the ladies de-bussed.

'Ah, man, man. That's a jaguar girl.'

'What you think, this girl?'

'At all.'

'She drink kellie-wellie?'

'Oh, man, I beg of you.'

My friendly Ghanaian guide explained as we were ushered into the reserved seats, 'Now, do not expect to see what you see in Europe or the UK. These ladies will be well clothed. Miss Northern Territory and Miss Trans-Volta will not be very lively; it is only Miss Western Territory who will do that. She has dance much High Life – this dance is very suggestive without meaning anything. But she has lives a carefree life. Maybe the judges do not like this.'

The entrants now came on the stage and the hall fairly rocked with a roar from the audience. Each young lady came up to the microphone against a backcloth inscribed 'Mass Education' and made a little speech to the assembled public. Miss Northern Territory was clad in a splendidly voluminous gown which was at the opposite pole from a western beauty queen's traditional bikini. Her actual figure remained a mystery. As my guide said, 'How difficult it is to decide on what we are to judge. Are we to cheer for our traditional type of beauty – a nice lady with comfortable fat? Or are we to go for your western type where everything is displayed, but is very thin?'

Miss Northern Territory was extremely traditional. She murmured softly into the mike, 'My name is Monica. I am seventeen years old and still at school. I have four brothers and

five sisters at home, just like me.' Then came the sensation –
Miss Trans-Volta Togoland. She had everything that the
Ghanaian wolves demanded: coffee-coloured skin, ample
areas of satiny flesh, and a smile like a row of pearls dropped
into a cup of chocolate. She started, 'My name is –' But it really
didn't matter what her name was; for the moment she had
scooped the kitty.

Miss Eastern Region, with the attractive name of Comfort,
tried to recapture interest with a potted biography: 'I am a
seamstress, and I live with my mother. I have been taught by
the Scottish missionaries.' In vain. No one could believe that
the worthy missionaries could have taught Miss Comfort what
girls learn easily in Togoland.

Chaos broke out in the halls as the audience clamoured to support their own favourite. A neutral Lebonese tried to suggest a compromise between Western and African standards of beauty: 'Why not judge on the proportions of the Venus de Milo?' There was a storm of protest, 'That lady is not in this competition.' Miss Upper-Volta Togoland rolled her generously proportioned figure, and swept everything before her. The prize was awarded to Ghana's own *'boule de suif'*, And quite right too!

Yes, let every country stick to its own standards and rejoice in the pleasures it creates for itself. The Beaujolais certainly did. It remained true to itself as Ghana did in its first beauty contest. My welcome everywhere was as fresh as the Beaujolais wine – one of the few good French red wines that you drink directly from the cellar, with no need to go through the ritual of bringing it up to room temperature. But as I pursued my increasingly rambling course through the Beaujolais vineyards, I became aware of a subtle change in the atmosphere of the war. Were the French, those masters of the swift-moving attack, beginning to slow down? I felt that I ought to slip across and see the Americans about this new situation. They were also involved in the joint plan for our advance from the south of France. With regret, I tore myself away from the fleshpots of the Clochemerle country, crossed the Saône and went up into the hills to seek out American headquarters.

When I dropped into the HQ of General Patch, near Besançon, I detected a slight anxiety among his staff. They gave me a briefing on the position as they saw it. As a war correspondent I had become a connoisseur of briefings and was fascinated by the difference in each Allied army's approach to this essential branch of the military art. Instinctively the British officer avoids the vivid word, wisely feeling that he can minimise the horror of war if he describes it in a jargon of his own. Sometimes that jargon can be distinctly puzzling to an outsider, especially if the briefing officer comes from the Brigade of Guards. After the rehearsal for the funeral of the late King George VI, a certain Guards colonel called his young officers together for a final pep talk. 'Good show,' he said, 'Good show. But remember, I want everything tickety-boo for the day of the race!'

I remember at Anzio listening to a British officer putting the Americans in the picture about a tank attack up the Albano road. He stood in front of a map on which every position was meticulously marked. 'Well, gentlemen,' he proceeded, 'our tins were hacking along the road with their swedes out of the lid when they got a bloody nose. The question is, shall we thicken up the party or do an Oscar? In any case, we'll have to tie the whole thing up on the old boy net.' Said one American anxiously to me, 'Thomas, are we advancing or are we retreating?'

The French method was in complete contrast. It naturally derived from the Napoleonic communiqué. Every statement had to be *'court, énergique et décisif'*. General de Lattre de Tassigny, standing before the French flag but with no map, explained how he pierced the Gap of Belfort. 'First, it was the optimism of the morning. Then it was the pessimism of the evening. And then, Messieurs of the Press, we consulted our final reports, and, *Pouf, c'était la victoire!*'

The Americans also believed in the swift punch line. When I discussed the problems of the Anvil landing with General Patch and asked how he proposed to solve them, he replied, 'In the American army, we don't solve our problems. We overwhelm them.' The American briefers certainly overwhelmed me. I always came out from a session with them slightly dizzy but boundlessly confident. Men who could make wisecracks with such effortless ease were obviously men of resource. As the officer told us before the breakout from the Anzio beachhead, 'General Mark Clark has got fifty-seven different plans and he's going to use every one of them.'

But at my briefing when I arrived from the Beaujolais, I

151

detected a slight lack of the usual buoyancy in the proceedings. General Patch might also have had fifty-seven different plans up his sleeve, but clearly he was a little uncertain about which one to use. After the briefing, a colonel on the staff – an old comrade-in-arms from the Anzio days – took me aside:

'You're going back to see the Frogs this afternoon, I hear?' Indeed, I had intended to go scouting through the vague no-man's-land of fifty miles which now separated the two armies. 'Well,' said the colonel thoughtfully, 'I wonder if you could give me your private opinion while you are there on a little problem that's got us kinda worried. I've got a feeling that the Frogs are doing a little bit of a go slow on us. I've got no proof. On paper, all's well. But in this game I've found that it's sometimes wise to back a hunch, and right now I've a hunch that our friends are staying a bit too long in this place Chalons something or other. Those babies can move all right when they want to.'

Chalons something or other. Obviously this was Châlons-sur-Saône. I felt that I already had a shrewd idea why the French were dragging their feet.

That evening I presented myself at the field HQ of General de Montsabert and received the usual warm welcome. The Intelligence Officer took me to the map tent and we reviewed the situation. There was no doubt that the enemy was retreating but the point was – how fast was he moving? What if he decided to fight a strong rearguard action before Dijon? Between Châlons and Dijon stretched the heart of Burgundy, the famous slopes of the Côte d'Or – the Golden Escarpment – covered with great vineyards. 'I need hardly tell you,' said my friend, 'the terrible consequences of such a decision. It would mean war, mechanised war, among the Grand Crus! Would France forgive us if we allowed such a thing to happen? We must not forget 1870.'

I confess that I had long ago forgotten what happened in Burgundy in 1870. But the colonel swiftly reminded me that one of the last battles of the Franco-Prussian war took place around Nuits-Saint-Georges. 'Shells fell on Les Cras. The German reserves swept forward over la Tâche, Romanée Conti and Richebourg. This must never be allowed to happen again.'

We both looked thoughtfully at the colonel's private map of the German positions. They were marked – quite properly – on the relevant sheet of Larmat's *Atlas Vinicole de la France*. There had been reports of Tiger tanks massing at Meursault and demolitions prepared at Chassagne-Montrachet. There might even be a strong German rearguard assembled behind Beaune. A picture immediately rose in my mind of air attacks on Vosne-Romanée, of smoke rising from the burnt-out château of Clos de Vougeot.

Then occurred one of those dramatic strokes that are the speciality of the French at war. A young *sous-lieutenant* entered, hurriedly saluted and, with a smile illuminating his face, declared, 'Great news, *mon colonel*, we have found the weak point in the German defences. Every one is on a vineyard of inferior quality.' We both recognised that we had reached a turning point in the battle. Said the colonel, 'General de Montsabert must know of this at once, but he will give only one order, *"J'attaque"*.'

Attack he did, and with such effect that in a matter of twenty-four hours the Germans were bundled out of Burgundy, and the French advance had jumped boldly ahead of the Americans. None of us can forget the glorious days that followed. *'Les Trois Glorieux'* at Dijon and in the Côte d'Or are yearly celebrated as a feast of wine and gastronomy. It was my privilege after the war to attend the famous sale of wines at the Hospice of Beaune, the feast of the Confrérie du Tastevin at the château of Clos de Vougeot and the *paulée*, the wine-growers' feast, at Meursault; but none of them could rival those fabulous three days of the Liberation of Burgundy. For a brief moment the cellar doors of the Côte d'Or opened almost of their own accord.

No wonder General de Montsabert's eyes sparkled as we raced up the Route National 74 in his jeep, close on the heels of his forward tanks. A blown bridge here, a demolished house there – what could these matter beside the great over-riding

fact of the undamaged vineyards stretching mile after mile before us.

To our left rose the long lines of the hills of the Côte; it was as if the Cotswold escarpment facing the Severn valley had been planted with vines and bathed in sunlight. 'Decidedly,' said the general, 'in the matter of wine if not in politics you must count me a man of the left.'

I must admit that, at this point, I lost touch with the advanced elements of the French army. A sound military maxim teaches the enlightened warrior that his first duty after victory is to make sure of his base. Accordingly I disappeared into the cellars of Beaune and Nuits-Saint-Georges to make certain that our objectives had remained undamaged. To my relief I found that the treasure house of the Côte had been untouched through the trials of war. The great *négociants* had learned from the experience of 1914-18. For in that war, as wine historians will recall, the wine men of France had been inexperienced in the tricks of resistance. André Simon related the sad story of a friend of his who was unpleasantly surprised to find that the advanced guard of the German army was rapidly approaching his priceless cellar. He made a quick decision. The only thing to do was to hide his great wines under the waters of the ornamental pond of the château. He had completed the bestowal of his treasures to the lake when the enemy arrived. All went well until the Germans walked out one morning to the lake to find the surface of the water covered with floating wine labels.

The Burgundians made no such mistake. They quickly spirited away their finest wines behind false walls in the depth of their cellars. A swift re-pasting of labels on inferior bottles convinced the ignorant conquerors that they were enjoying the great vintages of the Côte d'Or. The real treasures remained secure – until we arrived.

I have drunk great wines in many parts of France but never have I tasted such nectar in such quantities as was offered to me in the early days of the Liberation of Burgundy. The whole enchanted period in my life is a symphony of popping corks, through which the voices of the Cadets de Bourgogne reach me in the early days of the Liberation of Burgundy. That whole of the Corps de Chasse de St Hubert singing the theme song of Burgundian liberation, '*Toujours buveurs, jamais ivrognes!*'

But on the third day, as we tackled our twentieth cellar, my friend the colonel of Intelligence suddenly recalled that the outer world still existed. '*Les braves Amèricains,*' he declared, '*camarades anciens de la France. Il faut les envoyer quelques choses!*' Quickly my jeep was filled with some of the rarest treasures of the Côte. Outside one of the noblest cellars a little ceremony of historic importance was performed. A guard of honour saluted the departure of the great bottles destined for American consumption.

I drove my precious

jeep-load over the bumpy roads of La Bresse to the American HQ, now safely established in Besançon. Hurriedly I sought out my American contact and consigned the treasures to his care. All of them? Let me be honest: some of them, by an unaccountable chance of wartime transport, found their way to my cellar in the year after the war. Still, the bottles I handed over to the Americans were enough to make the fortune of any London restaurant in these over-priced years.

'These are the greatest wines of France,' I said with a flamboyant flourish. 'Guard them with care; rest them; then make certain they are *chambré* before they are served.'

'Don't worry,' the gallant US soldier reassured me, 'the Doc knows all about this Frog liquor. And while we are about it, we'll invite them over to drink it.'

So it was that in a certain eighteenth-century palace in Besançon the glories of the *belle époque* were splendidly revived.

The French guests advanced up flights of stairs lined on one side with the spahis from North Africa and on the other with the white-helmeted American military police, popularly known as Snowdrops. The American command awaited them in a salon worthy of a reception for Madame de Pompadour. Trumpets sounded, and a column of waiters marched in bearing the bottles on silver trays. My heart gave a warning thump – the bottles were from Burgundy and they were bubbling gently.

'We're in luck,' my American colonel whispered to me, 'the Doc's hotted up this stuff with medical alcohol!'

A look of incredulous horror flickered over the faces of the French. All eyes were turned on General de Montsabert. He had led them through the deserts of North Africa and over the snow-clad mountains of Italy. Faced with the greatest crisis so far in Franco-American relations, how would he behave? He fixed his staff with the stern glare of command, 'Gentlemen, take up your glasses.' Reluctantly the French reached out their hands. 'To our comrades in arms, *les braves Amèricains*,' he ordered in a ringing tone. He drained his glass with panache – every drop. Then, in a quieter voice that only the nearest Frenchmen and myself could hear, he murmured, 'Liberation, liberation, what crimes have been committed in thy name!'

The crimes, let me add, were the crimes of innocence. The United States – that generously hearted nation – produces good wines on its own account, but they are not the natural tipple of the average GI. And, come to think of it, would my Colonel have done any better? I, on the other hand, felt an excusable glow of superiority as I contemplated this final scene of Burgundian liberation. The south of France campaign had completed my vinous education, begun so long ago at Oxford and now brought to a triumphant conclusion in the cellars of Burgundy. I had been drinking at the fountainhead of wine knowledge. For weeks a succession of magnificent vintages had passed over my palate. Henceforth I would judge and pontificate with the best of them. To complete my pleasure, the French army awarded me the Croix de Guerre (*avec palmes*). Ostensibly, it was given for my frontline reporting of the French advance in Italy, but I knew better. It was surely an accolade for my conspicuous gallantry in the cellars of the Côte d'Or.

I shall remember those sensational Burgundies with deep affection. And why not? An old and noble wine is like a tried and trusted lover, say the French, but both must be enjoyed before it is too late. Or as the English put it:

> Time's wingèd chariot (poets say),
> Warns us to love while yet we may.
> Must I not hurry all the more
> Who find it parked outside my door,
> For those who sipped love in their prime
> Must gulp it down at closing time.

So, swift to the cellar. Let us end as we began, with a memorable bottle. We will decant it carefully, and certainly will not gulp it down. We will savour it with affection, for it will be a la Tâche 1944. Let us hail it as the Wine of Liberation.

INDEX

162